THE
DECORATED
DOLL HOUSE

JESSICA RIDLEY

How to Design and Create Miniature Interiors

Photographs by Norman Brand

Grove Weidenfeld

To my mother

ACKNOWLEDGMENTS

I would like to thank the following, who have helped me with this book:
Norman Brand, Colefax and Fowler, David Fletcher,
Jane MacAndrew, John Meek, Jane Rappeport, Susy Rickett,
Sophia Sackville West, Lucy Smith and
The Singing Tree for lending me their doll houses and furniture.

Published by Grove Weidenfeld
A division of Grove Press, Inc.
841 Broadway
New York, New York 10003-4793

Published in Canada by General Publishing Company, Ltd.

Library of Congress Cataloging-in-Publication Data

Ridley, Jessica.
    The decorated doll house/Jessica Ridley
        p. cm.
    ISBN 0-8021-1232-3
    1. Doll-houses. 2. Doll Furniture. 3. Miniature craft.
    I. Title.
    TT175.3.R54 1990   90-3933
    745.592'3--dc20   CIP

Conceived, designed, and produced by Toucan Books Limted, London

Manufactured in Italy by Arnoldo Mondadori

First American Edition 1990

10 9 8 7 6 5 4 3 2 1

Contents

INTRODUCTION

Decorating a doll house starts as a great hobby, but it soon becomes a raging addiction. I often wake up in the middle of the night suddenly realizing the answer to a particular problem and can't wait till the morning to try it out - how to make a pair of wall sconces, for example, or what to use for an Etruscan mosaic floor. Whatever the task, the challenge of getting each detail just right is immensely satisfying.

This all-embracing hobby will lead you down all sorts of new avenues - from carpentry through pottery, metal soldering and needlework to a crash course in decorative paint finishes. The scale of the house is what makes all this possible. You don't have to set aside a special work room, and if you do make a mistake it will be a very small one. All you need are a few basic tools and implements and various glues, paints and materials, but in such tiny quantities that it's worth buying the best quality; in fact, you can often get away with give-away samples. But be warned: you may become a compulsive hoarder of all sorts of unlikely things from bottle caps and scraps of plastic to pictures in magazines and aluminium foil - the range of uses you can put them to is amazing.

First, you need a doll house. These come in quite a range of styles and sizes which, in themselves, can suggest a theme for the interior. If you are starting from scratch, and buying a doll house, try to find one with interestingly-shaped rooms - rectangles at least, rather than plain square boxes - and consider the proportions of the rooms. In the end, choosing a doll house is rather like choosing a real house or apartment - you want to find one which offers the most scope for decoration.

Paint the outside of the house first, simply because it is easier to do this when the rooms are empty. Then do the hall, stairs and landings, and finally the rooms themselves. There is a tendency for doll houses to be decorated according to certain rather conventional and constricting codes - bulbous Victorian, for example, or reproduction Georgian, with a lot of dark varnished wood furniture and little color or elegance. Why? To me the joy of the whole game is to go further than that - to give the rooms as much character as you can possibly squeeze into ten or so inches square, and do it with a light touch and a sense of humor. There is no forbidden territory, so don't be afraid to experiment - after all, decorating a doll house is one of the best ways of expressing your imagination completely and freely.

This book is full of different styles of decoration, both historical and modern, together with contemporary interpretations of past fashions. Inspiration may come from real houses, museums, shops, photographs in books or magazines, or even from paintings. If you like a room, use it either as a starting point or make as faithful a copy as you can - including, even, a miniature version of your own house. Once you have chosen a style for a particular room, it is a good idea to do a bit of research - consult books or magazines in order to find out how a real room of this style would be furnished, what sort of drapes it should have and so on.

Most doll houses conform to a standard 1:12 scale. If you measure in inches, this makes life easy because 1 inch=1 foot. Furniture and objects can be scaled down to be exact replicas of their originals, but you must also judge the correctness of something by eye. Once you get used to looking at this scale, you will soon be able to tell instinctively whether an object placed in a room looks right, and if not, to try another. Taking a photograph of the room - a trick used by decorators of real rooms - to judge the correctness of their proportions, can help you to see what is wrong.

In some cases, achieving a substitute for a life-size object in miniature must rely on symbolism rather than accurate reproduction. So long as the eye perceives the object to be a miniature version of something it recognizes, the object will look good, even though it may not be made of the same material.

Wherever possible, things should work - doors should open and drapes should pull. But this approach can obviously not extend as far as stoves emitting heat or faucets gushing water, unless you are an expert boiler-maker or plumber. Lights that work are well worth the effort because they suddenly bring a room to life and let you see into its furthest corners. Real candles look good too, although they have to be changed rather frequently.

When deciding on a decorative style for a particular room, think of the overall color scheme because, when the front of the doll house is flung open, there should be a balance in tone and shade between the different rooms. You can either limit the scheme within each room to one predominant color or try using two contrasting colors - such as red and green or blue and yellow. Often just a little flash of a different color - on, say, a cushion or an ornament - can help to focus the eye and bring the room together.

Finding the last details - ornaments, sculptures, pictures and general props - is often the hardest but also the most enjoyable part of the game. Don't give in at the last minute to something inappropriate or to something which is out of scale. These finishing touches give the room the feeling of being lived in and used, and make the difference between a museum-piece and a really human doll house.

TOOLS AND MATERIALS

Paints

WOOD PRIMERS

This is an essential first coat of paint for new wood and previously varnished wood which is to be painted. Apply the primer to the wooden surface - this raises the grain and 'seals' the wood. When it is dry, sand it down lightly. The surface is then ready for painting with oil or water paints.

Spray primer
This is good for small things like moldings, picture frames and furniture. Use it sparingly and spray on several thin coats rather than one thick one which will drip and clog up the returns.

Spray primer is available in two colors - gray and white. If you have both colors, it is best to use white primer if the object is to be painted with pale colors, but gray if it is to be painted with darker colors such as black or brown.

Paint primer
Use this when you are priming the walls and ceilings of rooms or the façades of houses. Apply it evenly with a small house paintbrush and, when it is dry - it dries in approximately two hours - sand it down lightly. White is the most useful color because it can be used on its own, or it can be tinted with different-colored water-based paints (poster paint, gouache, watercolor). Primer can also be tinted and thinned with water to make a glaze. This is probably the most essential and versatile paint for doll house work.

WATER-BASED PAINTS

Emulsion
Use emulsion for painting walls and furniture, after they have been primed. Matt-finish emulsion looks best in doll houses. White is the most useful color because it can be tinted with water-based paints, but it is a good idea to buy small sample pots of darker colors, such as black.

Distemper
This is an old-fashioned house paint with a very flat, chalky appearance. It looks authentic in rooms which have a slightly old look but is less durable than emulsion. It can be tinted with water-based paints.

Both distemper and emulsion can be thinned and tinted to make a glaze for ragging, dragging, marbling, stenciling or woodgraining.

OIL-BASED PAINTS

Oil paints are more trouble to use because you need turpentine and oil colors to thin and stain them. They do, however, give a more authentic and professional finish to furniture and special effects such as woodgraining and marbling as the paint dries less quickly, thus giving you more time to work. They are also good for dying or tinting braid, cord and fabric.

Flat oil paint
This can be used as an undercoat/primer. It can also be thinned with turpentine or petroleum spirit and tinted to make a glaze.

Semigloss
This mid-sheen finish paint is particularly good as a second coat for moldings, woodwork, doors, windows and furniture. You can either use white semigloss tinted with oil colors or buy pots of different colored semigloss paint - again, small sample pots are a good size for doll houses.

CORRECTING MISTAKES

Stick masking tape around areas that you are not painting to keep them clean. If you make a mistake, remove oil paints with turpentine and water paints with a damp rag. Any chips or marks on the paintwork can be touched up with the original paint.

QUANTITIES

Mix oil paints in paper cups and water paints in plastic cups. Half a cup will easily cover one doll house room, but always keep the paint in case you need to touch up later on. If you cover the cup with plastic wrap the paint will last for quite a long time - a skin may develop on the surface, but if you pick this off the paint underneath will be fine. If you have kept the paint for a long time, you might need to thin it down with water (for water-based paints) or turpentine or petroleum spirit (for oil paints).

Varnishes

OIL-BASED VARNISH

This comes in matt, semigloss or gloss finishes. Use the appropriate finish for the effect you want. Woodwork looks smartest in semigloss, and furniture can be matt or semigloss. Thin the varnish with turpentine to make it easier to apply. You can also tint varnish with oil colors: for example, add raw umber to give an instant aged and distressed effect.

WATER-BASED VARNISH

This is used in the same way as oil-based varnishes. If you want to stain it, tint it with water-based paint.

ACRYLIC GLOSS VARNISH

This is used for coating construction paper to make stenciling paper. Apply it to both sides of the paper - it will make the paper waterproof - and leave to dry. The paper can then be cut into strips of stenciling paper.

SPRAY VARNISH

This is useful for varnishing small objects like moldings and furniture because it saves time. Apply it very lightly, so that it doesn't drip and clog up the returns.

Stainers

Both paints and varnishes can be tinted or stained to achieve a slightly aged effect. Use water or gouache colors to tint water-based paints and varnishes and oil colors to tint oil-based paints and varnishes. Use the earth colors (raw umber, burnt umber, raw sienna and burnt sienna) and black to tone down and distress bright colors.

WOOD DYES

These come in a range of woods and should be applied according to the instructions on the can. They can be used on furniture but the stain won't take on any areas that have been glued. Always test the color first on a part of the furniture that doesn't show, because these dyes act differently on different sorts of wood.

TEA

This is very useful for tinting white fabric, cord or braid. Make an infusion of whatever strength you need and, when it has cooled down dip the fabric in the tea. Do not use tea to stain delicate fabrics.

COFFEE

This can be used in the same way as tea, but it gives a stronger, warmer hue. Again, don't use on delicate fabrics.

ASH

This can be rubbed into surfaces to give an impression of dirt and age.

Adhesives and Tapes

Adhesives have a crucial role to play in decorating and furnishing doll houses. As you do more and more doll house work you will build up a selection for different jobs and materials. Tape and gripwax are also essential for positioning objects securely in rooms.

SPRAY MOUNT

This is good for light jobs like print rooms and, in a really thick layer, as a bed for mosaic or shell rooms, because it doesn't set. If it loses its stick it can be reactivated by a little heat - for example, place it near a heater, or warm it with a hairdryer.

PAPER GLUE AND FABRIC GLUE

These are all good for light jobs - sticking paper, construction paper, fabric, braid and so on - they stick well and do not leave a stain on the paper or fabric.

RUBBER GLUE

Use this for slightly tougher jobs such as upholstery, sticking pictures in frames, and for sticking balsawood.

WOOD GLUE

Use quick-drying wood glue, otherwise you have to hold things together while it dries. Wood glue works on hardwood, but not on balsawood. It will not, however, work on painted wood surfaces. Use wood glue for making wooden furniture. If the piece of furniture is going to be stained, use it sparingly so that it doesn't ooze out around the joins, because the stain will not take on the glued areas.

POLYVINYL ACETATE CONTACT GLUE (PVA)

This thermoplastic contact glue is one of the most useful and strong adhesives - it sticks wood, metal and plastic. PVA is also very versatile - it can be thinned down with water and used as a primer on styrofoam or polystyrene; and as a varnish with a very shiny finish; and it can be tinted with water paints and used as a colored varnish.

EPOXY RESIN GLUE

This is almost too strong for most doll house work, but it is useful for metal and shell furniture (see Grotto). Use the quick drying kind - this sets in a few minutes.

SUPERGLUE

Terrifying! Take great care not to get it on your fingers when you are doing small fiddly jobs. Only use it if the materials you are working with will not stick with any other adhesive - the styrene plastic for the units in the Modern Kitchen, for example.

WALLPAPER PASTE

You can use this for hanging wallpaper, in the same way as you would for a real room. Follow the instructions on the packet. It is, however, quite a messy way to hang wallpaper in doll houses - double-sided tape or PVA adhesive are easier to work with and just as strong.

MASKING TAPE

This is very useful for lots of temporary sticking jobs such as holding things in position while glue dries or sticking things to your cutting board to hold them firmly in position while you glue or solder them. It is also essential for masking off areas that you want to keep clean while you are painting. It can even be wrapped around miniature books and painted to give the impression of leather bindings.

DOUBLE-SIDED TAPE

This is one of the most useful materials for doll house work. Use it for hanging wallpaper - it is cleaner and easier than wallpaper paste; also, for battens when upholstering walls, for keeping carpets in place, and for sticking baseboards, dados and cornices onto walls. You will probably need both 1/2-inch and 1-inch tape.

GRIPWAX AND FLORAL CLAY

These are both used for holding objects securely in position in a finished room. Gripwax, which is sold in doll house shops, is stickier than Floral Clay and has the advantage of being colorless.

FIXING PADS

These double-sided adhesive pads (from DIY shops) are used for sticking pictures and mirrors to walls.

SOLDERING IRON AND WIRE

Use these for joining metal and wire. Try to buy wire which contains flux because it is easier to use. I also used thick solder wire to make the frame and legs for the black sofa and chairs in the Manhattan Living Room.

SILVER AND GOLD SCOTH TAPE

These are useful for trimming surfaces, such as the work surfaces in the Modern Kitchen.

══════ Paintbrushes ══════

SABLES

These fine-tipped brushes are expensive but they are essential for quality work. Sizes 0, 2 and 5 are probably sufficient for doll's house work - use them for decorating furniture and any detailed or delicate work.

HOG'S HAIR BRUSHES

These are stiff bristle brushes which are good for painting walls and woodwork. Buy flat, not rounded, brushes in sizes 6,8,10. Cut the ends off the handles if they are too long to fit into a room when you are painting it.

HOUSE PAINTBRUSHES

Use these for painting larger areas - the best sizes for doll house work are 1/2 and 1 inch.

FEATHERS

Goose or turkey wing-tip feathers from calligraphy shops or bird firms are essential for veining marble.

FAN BRUSH

This is not essential, but the widely splayed bristles are useful for wood-graining.

══ Wood and Moldings ══

Always keep a selection of strips of hardwood and balsawood of different thicknesses ranging from $1/32$ to $1/4$ inch. Use hardwood for making furniture because it is heavier and more durable. Balsawood is easier to cut into rounded or curved shapes, but it is very fragile and light.

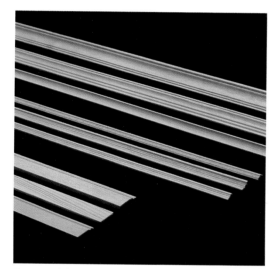

Buy moldings from doll house shops. There are various grades of baseboards, dado rails, cornices, window and door frames as well as picture frame and mirror frame moldings. Use plain single moldings for simple country rooms, and deeper, more elaborately carved ones for grander rooms.

Also keep a selection of dowel and square section lengths, cocktail sticks and bamboo kebab or satay skewers. These come in handy for making all sorts of things from table legs, plate racks and hat stands to fences and gate posts.

CRAFT KNIFE AND SCALPEL

These are both essential tools for cutting all sorts of materials including polystyrene, paper, cardboard and even balsawood. Keep the blades very sharp for a clean cut. Use a metal ruler to cut against - if you use a wooden or plastic ruler the blade will cut into the edge of the ruler.

MINIATURE MITER BOX AND SAW

A miniature miter box and saw are essential tools for doll house woodwork. You can buy them from miniaturist and hobby shops and suppliers.

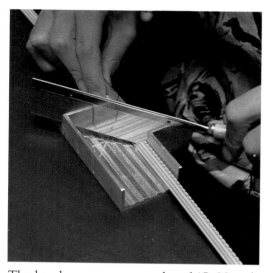

The box has grooves at angles of 45, 90 and 135 degrees which enable you to cut wood and moldings to the correct angle. The blade of the saw should have 32 teeth per inch. Use your miter box and saw to cut exact 90-degree angles when you are making furniture and to miter the ends of moldings at 45-degree angles so that they fit into the corners of rooms.

SANDPAPER

Fine to very fine grades are the most useful for doll house work. Beware of over-sanding a straight piece of wood and wearing it away at the edges. To avoid this, lay the sandpaper on a flat surface and rub the piece of wood along it rather than holding the sandpaper in your hand. Using sandpaper is often an easy way to achieve smooth curved cuts in the wood - cut with a saw or craft knife outside your guide line and sand down to the exact size required. Sandpaper is also a good means of achieving an old, distressed look on furniture; after painting, simply rub sandpaper along the grain of the wood and take off some of the paint. Rub more away in areas which would have had the most wear - such as table edges or the arms of chairs.

MINIATURE HARDWARE

Doll house suppliers sell special miniature nails, screws and hinges which are always useful. You can use very small picture hanging rings and screw-eyelets for putting up curtain poles.

Lighting

Doll house shops sell kits for electrifying your doll house. They work with an adapter plugged into the mains. Decide where to place the lights before you start decorating the rooms so that you can drill any necessary holes in the walls for the wires. Try to conceal the wires under carpets and behind wallpaper where possible. Think carefully about what sort of lights you want for a particular room - like the furniture, they must be in keeping with the style of the room. For example, use chandeliers for grand rooms, table lamps or standard lamps for more comfortable rooms and spotlights and uplighters for modern rooms. If you cannot buy exactly the right lamp for your room, make your own (see page 37). Although lighting a room is quite fiddly, it is well worth the effort because it really does bring a room to life.

Fabrics

I find that I use a surprisingly wide range of fabrics and have a huge hoard of little scraps.It is often very hard to tell which one will look right both in scale and color in any given room without holding it in the room first to see how it looks. Generally, it is best to use natural fabrics rather than synthetics in doll houses because they are easier to work with, they hang better, and always look more realistic in a room.

For drapes, natural lightweight fabrics are best - cotton lawn or gingham - while silk, crepe de chine, pure silk lining material and Indian chiffon are best for net curtains. All these fabrics contract into natural gathers when they are dampened, and therefore hang well. If you are making formal pleated drapes you can get away with thicker fabrics such as chintz. Sew the drapes with the thinnest possible thread or with invisible nylon thread - I usually do this by machine as it looks neater and smarter, although curtain rings do have to be sewn on by hand. Because doll house drapes are made with such lightweight fabrics, they nearly always have to be weighted to make them hang well. To do this, sew lead curtain weights or fishing weights into the bottom hems. Before hanging drapes in a room, it is also a good idea to hold them over the spout of a boiling kettle - the steam dampens them and helps to make them limp and less bouncy. Hang them when they have dried.

Upholstery fabrics need not be quite so thin - indeed there is a risk of glue creeping through them if they are. Chintz, cottons, silk, taffeta and woven patterned fabrics are all suitable. Try to find fabrics with the right pattern and color for a particular room rather than worrying about the weight of the cloth. Liberty and Provençal prints work well, so do very fine checks and stripes. To make piping braid, use fine cord and tint it with tea or dye it in watercolor inks or oil colors to the right color. Very fine picot braid, from the notions counter, is good for edging short chair covers, drapes and drapery tie-backs.

Cushions can be made from scraps of silk. Either use printed fabric, or paint pictures or patterns onto plain silk with oil colors. Trim the cushions with the same braid that you have used for the chairs.

Carpets, mats and rugs can be made from a wide range of fabrics. Velvet makes good pile carpets - use cotton velvet or silk velvet if possible. If you want to make a patterned rug you can draw the design onto velvet with felt pens - use pale colors for a subtle faded effect. Or you can cut the velvet into animal shapes and paint on stripes or spots to make tigerskin or leopardskin rugs. Stick them on a slightly larger piece of green or red felt to make them look more authentic. Velvet ribbon is perfect for stair carpets because, if you can buy the right width for your stairs, it is already hemmed and you can simply glue it in place. (Make stair rods from hair pins or cocktail sticks with a tiny bead stuck on each end.) Felt makes very good wall-to-wall carpets, it is easy to work with and it doesn't fray. Burlap, tinted with strong tea, makes a good substitute for coir or rush matting.

Scraps of fabric also come in handy for lots of little jobs - making sheets and pillowcases for a bedroom, towels for the bathroom and hats for the hat shop - you can even use tapestry-backing, tinted with tea or coffee as a substitute for wickerwork.

Modeling Materials

MARBLEX AND DAS

These are fine modeling clays which harden when they dry out. Keep it cool and damp when you are not using it. Use this clay to make plates, cups and saucers, bowls, jugs, vases and sinks. It takes about 24 hours to dry out completely and set hard. Work reasonably quickly, and dampen your fingers occasionally to keep the clay moist - if it starts to dry out you will not be able to mold it well and it is liable to crack. If you are making a sink or handbasin, roll it out with a rolling pin and cut slabs to fit round a mold, then dampen the edges to join them together. Remove the mold after a few hours. When it is dry, tidy up your work if necessary by sanding it down with very fine grade sandpaper and smoothing down any lumps and bumps.

Air-dry clay is available in two colors, white and terracotta, but it can be painted with water colors or gouache, which sink into the porous surface well. When the paint is dry, apply a coat of varnish to bring up the colors of the paint. Use gloss varnish to achieve an enamel or porcelain effect.

FIMO

Fimo is a modeling clay which is hardened by baking for about 15 minutes in a low-temperature oven. It is not quite as easy to work with as air-dry clay, but it is the best material for making miniature flowers and food. First you need to activate it by kneading it in your fingers for a few minutes. Then mold it into shape and bake it. If, when you are molding it, the Fimo becomes too soft to work easily, cool it off in the freezer or fridge for a few minutes.

Fimo comes in a great range of colors. You can blend the colors together and add white or transparent Fimo to lighten them. Or you can just buy white Fimo and paint it after you have molded and baked your object - this can be fiddly on such a tiny object, but it is more economical. Use oil colors to paint Fimo, and apply a coat of gloss varnish if desired.

When you start working with Fimo, begin by making simple things, such as eggs or carrots, before going onto more fiddly and complicated things like flowers. Making food and flowers is time-consuming, but it is well worth the effort. Food on a dining-room table or vases of flowers in a drawing room are perfect finishing touches; they help bring the room to life and give the impression of being lived-in.

Furniture

Doll house shops do sell a wide range of furniture varying from cheap Taiwanese imports to very beautiful, but expensive, handmade English pieces. Go for the best shapes of whatever furniture you need, making sure that the proportions of the piece are right for the room. The imported range tends to be covered in a thick, toffee-apple like varnish, which looks rather extraordinary. This is fine for painting over: apply one coat of primer and then apply either semigloss or emulsion, tinted to whatever color you like. Then you can pick out the moldings or decorate it as you wish. Raw wood furniture can be stained with wood dyes or oil colors to tone down its new look and make it settle into its surroundings.

It is very important to find exactly the right pieces of furniture for any particular room, because they are part of the character of that room. A Louis XV chair is not going to look particularly happy in the Nursery or the Scottish Baronial Hall, for example. If you are not quite sure how a certain type of room should be furnished, have a look at photographs in books and magazines for inspiration. You can also pick up ideas by looking at real rooms. If you cannot find exactly what you want in a doll house shop, you can make your own pieces.

Making your own furniture is not as difficult as it sounds, provided you have a selection of hardwood strips and moldings, a fine-tooth saw and miter box and some quick-drying wood glue. The advantage is that you can make exactly the piece you want to fit into a particular space. When working out how to make the piece, be very accurate with your measurements - on such a small scale, a mistake of $1/8$ inch looks very big. Try to avoid getting glue all over the wood, other than the bits that are being stuck together, because if you intend to dye or stain the wood, the stain will not take on these glued areas.

Start off by making simple pieces - a bookcase or a simple table - before going on to more complicated side tables and chairs. Paint or stain the piece to suit the style of the room and distress it by rubbing off some of the paint with sandpaper if you want it to look old and worn.

There are, however, some items which are almost impossible to make, and are therefore worth investing in - these might include a bathtub and basin for a bathroom, a grate for a fireplace, a cast iron stove for a kitchen, and brass chandeliers wired up for electricity for formal rooms.

TREASURE YOUR TRASH

When you are decorating and furnishing your doll house, you will find that your powers of ingenuity and inventiveness will really be put to the test. Sometimes you will not be able to buy exactly the right piece of furniture for a particular room, and will therefore want to make your own. What, for example, can you use to make a standard lamp or a black leather sofa and chairs? Although it can take days to come up with a solution, it is always worth waiting until you find exactly the right material to make any particular object.

The first thing that you will learn is never to throw anything away - it is quite extraordinary what you can make out of old bits of rubbish. Corks and bottle caps, cocktail sticks, aluminium foil, old felt-tip pens - all these normal everyday bits and pieces can be used to make convincing miniature accessories.

If you are really stuck for the solution to a problem, scour the shelves of a DIY emporium. There are masses of extraordinary materials - tapes, tubes, polystyrene and so on - which can be used. This is how I found the self-adhesive insulation foam for the black leather chairs in the Manhattan Living Room and the polystyrene coving for the barrel-vaulted ceiling in the Yellow Drawing Room.

Finally, don't despair if something doesn't work first time. It is only by experimenting that you will find out how certain materials will work, and how they will look in a finished room.

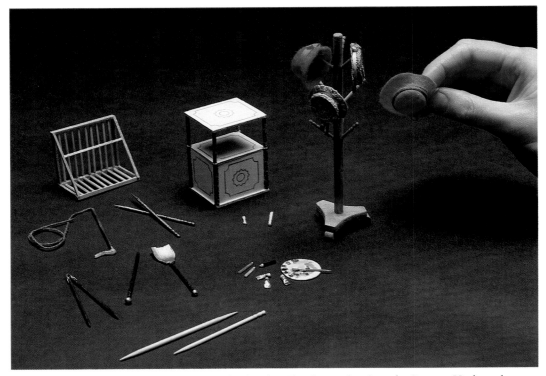

These accessories have all been made with cocktail sticks. The plate rack is from the Country Kitchen; the whip, spears, poker, shovel and fire tongs are all from the Scottish Baronial Hall; the bedside table is from the English Country-House Bedroom; the hatstand is from the Hat Shop and the miniature paintbrush and crayons with the palette are from The Studio at Charleston.

Bottle caps, corks and small kitchen or medicine measures have been used to make vases, a trefoil pouf for the Yellow Drawing Room, metal chairs for the Manhattan Living Room, and a bowl in the microwave oven. Corks have also been used as a base for making hats, and bottle caps as a base for making quiches and pies.

Jewelry findings are incredibly useful for making all sorts of metal accessories. Here, for instance, they have been used to make a range of kitchen utensils for the Modern Kitchen; an earring clip forms the base of a candle sconce for the Colonial Dining Room; a brooch backing is used as a breakfast tray for the English Country-House Bedroom and so on.

THE PROJECTS

The rooms and façades in this book are decorated in a wide range of styles, and incorporate a number of different techniques. The rooms are grouped together according to their type: formal rooms; eating rooms; bedrooms and bathrooms; shops; work and play rooms or 'dens'. Within each section, the first room is the easiest to decorate and furnish, and after that they become progressively more difficult. Don't expect to become an expert decorator overnight - so if you have never decorated or furnished a bedroom, it is better to start on the Scandinavian Bedroom rather than the English Country-House Bedroom.

If you are attempting something for the first time it is always a good idea to experiment first so if, for example, you are trying a new painting technique, try it out first on a piece of lightweight cardboard or a piece of wood which has been primed - and don't give up in a huff if it doesn't work first time. With a little practice and plenty of patience, you will be able to master all the skills required to decorate a truly stunning doll house.

Don't feel that you have slavishly to follow all the decorative schemes that I have used - use them as a starting point and modify them to suit your doll house. Pick out certain features from one room and adapt them to suit another. You could, for example, transport the marble floor in the Manhattan Living Room into the Modern Kitchen. Whatever the type of room you chose to decorate and furnish, it is always worth doing a little background research into the style before you start. Find out exactly what sort of lamps are suitable, and what sort of floor covering will suit the style of the room. In the end, getting all these little details absolutely right is what makes the room look convincing.

Finally, whatever you are making or decorating, do always bear in mind the 1:12 doll house scale - wallpaper with a pattern that is too big or a piece of furniture that is too large will always stand out in a finished room, and distort the overall impression of that room.

*The blank façade of a doll house
provides the canvas on which you
can paint any number of period details.
This one became the
Italian Villa on page 68.*

CHINESE ROOM

Western imitations of Chinese art became very fashionable during the eighteenth century. Under the rococo influence, however, Chinoiserie - as this subdued exoticism was known - developed into a style more whimsically elegant than anything produced in China. Dragons, strange birds and fantastic Chinese landscapes with pagodas were painted on walls, or porcelain, and woven into silks and tapestries. The style relies heavily on the use of red lacquer, black lacquer and gold which create an immediately striking impression, particularly in miniature.

Walls Decorated in the Chinese Style

1 Take a sheet of newspaper and cut it into pieces that fit each of the walls. Hold each one against the appropriate wall and mark the exact dimensions of the wall together with the positions of any doors and windows. Then cut around these features to create a template for each wall.

2 Take a sheet of bright red, medium-weight construction paper. Place each of the four templates on top of it, in turn, and cut around the edges of the template. Each of these red sheets will now correspond to a wall of the room.

3 Pencil a horizontal line across each sheet of red paper at the height of the bottom of the window - this indicates the position of the dado rail. Next, decide the size and position of each of the black panels above the dado rail. The architecture of the room will help determine their arrangement. In this case, there were two windows at the front so I penciled a narrow panel beside each of these; on one of the sides, I placed a large panel next to the door and one little panel above it; on the back, where there are no architectural features, there was room for three panels; and on the fourth side, which is similarly bare of features, I decided to place one panel on either side with a gilded mirror frame in the middle. When penciling the position of the black panels, always leave about ³/8 inch from the edges of the room and about ¹/4 inch either side of the dado rail.

4 Pencil the positions of the horizontal panels that will run below the dado rail.

5 Then, cut out all the vertical panels from a sheet of medium-weight black construction paper.

6 Take some acrylic gold paint and tone this down with raw umber and black gouache to give an impression of age. Then, begin to paint Chinese motifs on each of the black panels. Inspiration might come from pictures of Chinese furniture or from the motifs on a willow-pattern plate. If, however, you find the idea of freehand decoration daunting at first, you could always make a tracing from a suitable image that has been photo-copied and reduced to the correct scale. But always remember that Chinese decoration of this sort is highly stylized and, hence, very simple: the trees have gnarled trunks and the branches curve right over, giving the impression of stunted growth. Hold the brush upright to give you better control and begin at the bottom, moving up the trunk and out along each leaf with one stroke, lifting your brush lightly as you move away from the base so that it tapers away towards the tip.

7 When you have finished a Chinese picture for each of the black panels, stick the panels into position on the sheets of red construction paper with rubber glue.

8 Take a piece of shiny gold lightweight cardboard and cut it into strips about ¹/8 inch wide, using a craft knife. These will form the frames of the black panels. Then cut the strips into lengths which correspond to the top and bottom sides of the panels. Miter each end with a 45-degree angle and stick the lengths into position with rubber glue or double-sided tape.

9 Create the impression of moldings on the frames by scoring two lines with a pencil. Make a dado rail from a strip of gold cardboard ⅛ inch wide, score it and stick it onto the red paper.

10 Using a gold felt-tip pen, trace over the pencil lines which mark the panels below the dado rail. Add a second set of gold lines to each panel to create the illusion of an inset panel.

=========== **Marble Floor** ===========

1 The idea for this floor came from a print in a magazine. I then enlarged it on a photocopier to fit the scale of the room.

2 On threepieces of lightweight cardboard, create three colored marbles, ranging in intensity from light to dark (see page 40).

3 Using the photocopy as a reference, pencil onto each of the pieces of cardboard a grid of identical shapes: diamonds on one sheet and parallelograms on the other two. Then, cut them out.

4 Take a thicker piece of cardboard and apply rubber glue to it. Stick the shapes onto this, gradually building a mosaic of marble chips. Butt the edges tightly together but don't let them overlap.

5 When you have finished assembling the mosaic, take a piece of newspaper and create a template of the floor of the room. Place the template on top of the mosaic and trim around the edges so that it is the correct size. With a soft brush, apply a thick coat of gloss polyurethane varnish to the mosaic floor, which will help to fill in any cracks between the marble tiles.

=========== **Decorating a Chest of Drawers** ===========

1 Remove the handles and smooth the chest of drawers with sandpaper. Apply a coat of black or very dark green semigloss paint to all but the top of the object. Paint the top with white semigloss. The piece of furniture is now ready for marblizing.

2 Place squeezes of raw umber, burnt sienna and black onto the side of a plate and pour some flat white paint and a little turps or petroleum spirit into the middle. Then mix a browny gray glaze and apply it to the top of the chest of drawers with a small sable brush. Make sure that you paint around the edges, as well as the top, because the end-result should resemble a single slab of marble. Leave the glaze for a minute in order to let it set.

3 Next, take a cotton rag and dab it gently over the surface to create a textured background.

4 Dip a goose feather into the original glaze on the plate and mix in varying amounts of extra black and raw umber to make it darker. Fidget the feather lightly across the surface, building up a network of veins as you go. Make sure that some of the veins run right over the edge of the top of the chest of drawers.

5 The final stage of this process is to splatter the surface of the top with drops of the darker mixture (step 4), adding a little burnt sienna this time. Holding the sable brush with the hand that you normally use for painting, pull the index or middle finger of the other hand back through the bristles of the brush, spraying the surface with fine droplets of glaze. Leave to dry.

Assembling the Room

1 Apply PVA adhesive to the back of the red Chinese wallpaper and stick it onto the walls. Make sure that you push the paper right into the corners of the room and smooth out any bubbles or creases in the paper. Attach the door frame after you have done this since it goes on top of the wallpaper.

2 Apply PVA adhesive to the back of the floor and stick it into the room, making sure that you push it right into the corners.

In keeping with the formality of the room, I decided that the furniture should be simple, sparse, classical and rich. And so, I covered the chairs with scarlet silk and transformed a bombé chest of drawers (bombé literally means 'blown-out' and refers to the swelling shape given to the fronts of rococo chests of drawers). I painted this to create the effect of black lacquer, picked out with touches of gold, and gave it a false marble top.

SCOTTISH BARONIAL HALL

The idea here is to create a slightly old and battered Scottish hall. The bare stone walls are covered with chicken wire which is hung with hunting trophies, chain mail suits and a vast array of weaponry. The furniture, which is quite big and chunky, is rather worn - in keeping with the look of the room. All these elements give the room a remote and distinctly feudal feel.

Walls, Ceiling and Floor

1 Apply a coat of white primer to the walls and ceiling. Leave to dry. Sand them down lightly, and apply a coat of matt white emulsion. Leave to dry.

2 Stick masking tape around the edges of the ceiling, door and window frames to keep them clean while painting the walls.

3 Mix some white emulsion with water on a metal plate until it has a milky consistency. Tint with raw umber, black and brilliant yellow gouache colors to make a pale stone-colored glaze. Test the color on the wall - if it is not right, wipe it off quickly with a rag and adjust it. When you are satisfied with the color, apply the glaze to one of the side walls, thinly and quickly - don't worry if the brush marks show.

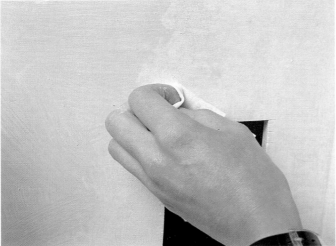

4 While the paint is still wet, take a pad of cotton rag and dab it all over the wall, removing the paint as you go. Keep the pad of rag fairly flat so that the pattern which emerges is quite subtle, and be sure to push the rag right into the corners.

5 Repeat steps 3 and 4 on the other two walls, one at a time, ragging each wall as soon as it has been painted.

6 Paint the mantelpiece with the same stone-colored glaze and rag it, making sure that the rag gets into all the moldings.

7 Thin the glaze with some more water, and darken it by adding a little more black. Dab the cotton pad into this darker paint and then dab it roughly onto the walls, especially at the top of the room, and around the fireplace where the walls will be dirtier and smoke-stained. Keep twisting the pad in your hand so that the pattern is not repeated.

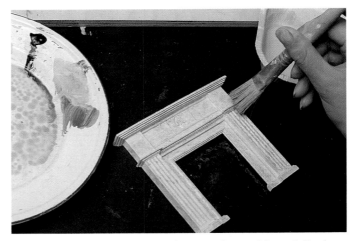

8 Dab this darker paint onto the mantelpiece. If it is difficult to get the rag in between the moldings, use a small brush.

9 The next stage is to draw in the edges of the stone slabs. It is best to use a pencil for this as it is the right color and any mistakes can be rubbed out.

10 A good size for the slabs is 3/4 inch high and 2 inches wide, although this obviously depends on the size of the room you are decorating. Draw in the first horizontal line at the height of the top of the mantelpiece. Use the mantelpiece instead of a ruler for this, moving it around the room.

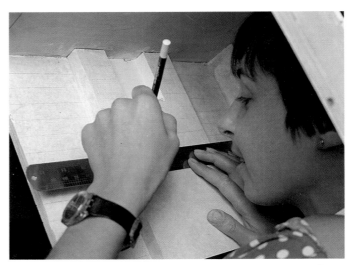

11 Then, using a pencil and ruler, make marks on each wall every 3/4 inch above and below this line. Join the marks using a ruler and a 2H pencil, to give the horizontal lines all the way round the room.

12 Next, mark the walls for the positions of the vertical lines. Although the stone slabs are 2 inches wide, you will need to mark the wall at 1-inch intervals because they will be laid like a brick wall. Using a ruler and pencil, fill in the first vertical line on alternate horizontal strips. Move the ruler to the next mark and fill in vertical lines on the other horizontal strips. Repeat this process around the room, to give the effect of a stone wall.

13 Paint the area behind the fireplace with matt black emulsion. When dry, stick the fireplace onto the wall with PVA.

14 Take strips of cornice and baseboard, and cut them into lengths which correspond to the lengths of the walls. Miter the ends of the cornice and baseboard that will fit into the corners of the room, using a miniature miter box and saw (see page 11). Apply a coat of white primer. Leave to dry.

15 Mix a slightly off-white paint, consisting of white emulsion tinted with raw umber gouache. Apply a coat to all the strips of cornice and baseboard, and also to the door. Leave to dry.

16 Stick the cornice onto the top of the walls with wood glue. Place the door in the door frame.

17 For the carpet, take a piece of tartan fabric; the checks of the tartan should be small, about 1/2 inch, to fit the scale of the room. Cut the material to the exact size of the room. Place it in the room and carefully cut round the door frame, mantelpiece and chimney breast. Cover the floor with a thin layer of fabric glue or rubber glue, and lay the carpet into the room, pushing it right up against the walls and into the corners. Stick the baseboards onto the walls with wood glue, pushing them down firmly, to keep the carpet flat.

'Chicken Wire', Armour and Weapons

The 'chicken wire' is made from tulle, bought in any fabric shop. It will be hung on each wall from the ceiling to the height at which a dado would be placed about 2 1/2 inches from the floor. The tulle on the wall above the fireplace will hang from the ceiling to the top of the mantelpiece. Above the door it will hang from the ceiling to the top of the door frame.

1 Measure each wall and cut pieces of netting that are the same width as the wall but about 1/2 inch longer than the height. Fold over 1/4 inch of the tulle at the top and bottom of each piece and hem with colorless nylon thread.

2 Put the tulle onto a piece of paper and paint or spray it with gray acrylic paint to give it a metallic look. Leave to dry.

3 Take several thin brass rods (which can be bought at hobby shops) and, with a pair of scissors, cut them into lengths that correspond to the width of each piece of 'chicken wire'. You will need two rods for each piece of tulle - top and bottom.

4 When the tulle is dry, thread the rods through the hem. The top one will be for hanging the tulle and the bottom one will act as a weight to keep the material straight.

5 To make the weapons to hang on the chicken wire, use large buttons for shields, plain wooden cocktail sticks for spears and plastic sword-shaped cocktail sticks for swords. Apply a thick coat of gray acrylic to all these, using an old paintbrush.

6 To make stag's and moose's heads, buy a selection of plastic animals from a toy store and simply cut their heads off about halfway down the neck with a small saw or craft knife.

7 To make the heads look less plasticky, take two pieces of finely woven cotton velvet - one dark brown and one pale brown. Fray the edges, and collect all the loose frayed bits of cotton in a little pile. Apply a coat of clear semigloss varnish to the stag's head and antlers, avoiding the eyes and mouth. Stick the velvet frayings onto the varnished head, but not the antlers. The heads will now have a furry, slightly moth-eaten look.

8 Dip the antlers into a bag of rottenstone powder (wholemeal flour is a good substitute). Gently blow off any excess.

9 On a piece of tracing paper, draw a shield shape and transfer it to a small piece of hardwood 1/8 inch thick. Using a craft knife, cut around this shape. Smooth down the curves with sandpaper if necessary. Stain the shields with a dark wood-stain.

10 Stick the stags' heads onto the shields with wood glue.

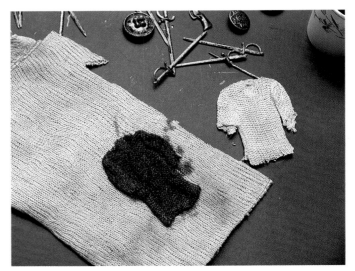

11 To make a chain-mail suit from an old-fashioned knitted dishcloth, cut out two body shapes and sew them together, with the purled sides together. Turn the suit inside out, so that the purled side is on the outside. Paint it with gray acrylic paint.

12 Distress the weapons, shields and chain-mail suits by applying a coat of clear semigloss varnish tinted with raw umber and black oil-colors.

13 Attach the weapons, shields, stags heads and chain mail to the chicken wire either with PVA glue, or by sewing them on with colorless nylon thread. I have arranged the swords in a large circle around a shield on one of the walls, and stuck stags' heads around the top of each piece of chicken wire.

Draperies

Make the drapes from fine cotton or silk. Try to avoid using synthetic fabrics because they don't hang very well.

1 Measure the width of the window, including the window frame, and the height from the top of the window frame to the floor. The width of each drape will be double the width of the window and the height will be from the top of the window frame to the floor, with an extra inch added for hemming.

2 Cut out the drapes. Fold over about 1/4 inch on each side of the curtains and hem them.

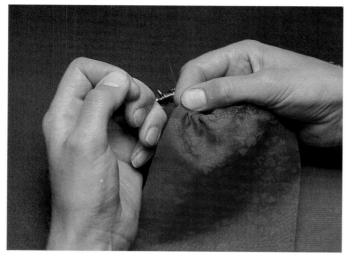

3 Hem the top of each drape with a double line of machine stitching, and leave the ends loose. Pull the threads to gather the drapes to the right width at the top, and secure the loose ends.

4 Use small jewelry jump rings as curtain rings. Sew the rings onto the back of the drape at the top at intervals of 1/4-1/2 inch.

5 Peel off the coating of a strip of small curtain weights. Cut the strip of weights to fit the drapes. Hem the bottom of the drapes, with the curtain weights inside the hem.

6 Thread the curtain rings onto a brass rod.

7 Mark the position of the curtain rail on the wall and, with a bradawl, make holes at the points where the rail will be attached. Screw in two small screws with eyelets or loops at the end and hang the curtain rail and drapes between them.

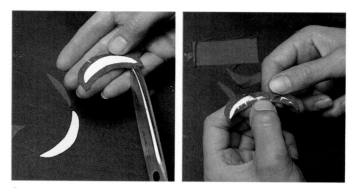

8 Draw two crescent shapes on a piece of lightweight cardboard and cut them out. These will be the basic shape for the tie-backs. Place the crescents on a piece of drape fabric, and cut the fabric into similar shapes, but about 1/4 inch larger all the way round. Fold the fabric over the cardboard and glue it onto the other side. You might need to cut little nicks on the concave side of the fabric to make it fit smoothly over the cardboard.

9 Trim the tie-backs by sticking some braid, painted to match the drapes, on the convex side of the tie-back.

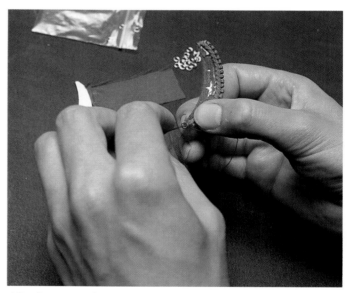

10 Sew a jewelry jump ring onto each end of the tie-backs.

11 Make two small holes in the wall, with a bradawl, where the tie-backs will hook onto the wall. Hammer in two small hooks. Tie the drapes back and loop the rings onto the hook.

Assembling the Room

When everything is attached to the chicken wire, it can be nailed to the walls. Mark the positions of the nails on the wall - just below the cornice. Make small holes in these positions with a bradawl. Use a small hammer and tiny nails which can be bought from craft shops. Put the nails through the tulle and hammer into the wall just below the cornice. Furnish the room with a large table, chairs, and anything else you think is appropriate. I made an umbrella stand by painting the top of a lipstick case with oil paints, and put a few sticks, made out of twigs, in it. The tigerskin rug was made by cutting out a piece of cotton velvet in a tiger shape, and painting the tiger pattern onto it.

Make the hall look really lived-in by leaving hats and scarves on the table, and a few magazines or newspapers on the floor.

PRINT ROOM

Print rooms became fashionable in English houses during the second half of the eighteenth century when engraving was the only method of reproducing paintings. Prints were stuck directly onto the walls of a room, and decorated with borders, bows and other ornaments. This one is painted a very old-fashioned blue which has yellowed with age and woodsmoke. The slightly formal furniture is in keeping with the eighteenth-century style and the room is simply lit by a three-arm chandelier.

Walls and Ceiling

1 Apply white primer to the walls and ceiling and leave to dry.

2 Paint the ceiling with white emulsion. Leave to dry.

3 Paint the area behind the fireplace with matt black emulsion.

4 Before painting the walls it is a good idea to stick masking tape around the black fireplace, and along the edges of the ceiling; this will keep the edges clean while you are painting the walls a different color.

5 Mix a grayish-green paint consisting of white matt finish emulsion tinted with small quantities of cobalt, viridian, yellow and raw sienna gouache. Test the color on the wall before painting - if it is not right, wipe it off with a damp rag.

6 Starting on one of the side walls, apply the paint generously, but evenly, with a small house paintbrush or a hog's hair brush. Work your way around all the walls, taking care not to allow any drips or ridges to form. Leave to dry overnight. If the white undercoat shows through when it is dry, apply a second coat.

7 Marble the fireplace (see page 37).

8 Cut lengths of baseboard to fit the walls and miter the ends. Apply a coat of white primer. Leave to dry, and put on one side.

The prints in print rooms tend to be of one subject, for example, architectural or botanical or landscapes. Once you have decided on a theme you should start looking around for suitable prints. Illustrations in magazines, auction house and art gallery catalogues are the best places to find them. You will need quite a large selection; try to find as many different shapes as possible - some round or oval ones, as well as portrait and landscape rectangles.

9 Either cut out the prints, or photocopy them and cut out the copies, leaving a border of about 1/4 inch all the way round the print - this is where the frame will be stuck. If a picture in a magazine is too big, you can reduce the size on a photocopier.

10 The frames are made by finding pictures of borders in découpage books and reducing them to the right size - just less than 1/4 inch wide - on a photocopier. You will need different borders so that the frames are not all the same. Cut out the border, and stick it around the picture, cutting the ends of each edge at 45 degrees so that they look mitered.

11 The dado rail and cornice are also made by photocopying borders. Cut them into lengths that fit the walls of the room.

12 You will also need reduced photocopies of swags and ribbons to decorate the walls. These can be copied from decorators' catalogues or magazines.

13 Cut out a paper template of each wall of the room. Spray a thin layer of Spray Mount adhesive onto the paper. Stick the dado rail on to the paper 2 inches above the level of the floor - this will act as a guideline when you position the pictures.

14 Arrange the prints on the template to give yourself an idea of how they will look when they are in the room - if you are unhappy with the positions, peel them off and rearrange them. The prints should be hung all over the walls from the ceiling right down to the dado - don't be afraid to hang some of the bigger prints right at the top of the room - they will look more imposing. Try to find pairs of pictures to hang together, and vary the shapes and sizes. Stick down the swags, bows and ribbons between the prints - just above or just below them.

15 Stick the cornice into the room with Spray Mount. Draw a pencil line 2 inches from the floor all around the room, and stick the dado onto this line. Stick the fireplace into position with double-sided tape or PVA adhesive.

16 When all the prints are in position on the templates, turn each print over, keeping it in the same position. When they are all face down, spray another thicker layer of Spray Mount onto the backs of the prints. Then, place each print onto the wall in the position that corresponds to its position on the template. Ensure that the prints are straight before you stick them down.

17 To give the room a really authentic old and slightly dirty look, apply a coat of tinted varnish. Pour some semigloss varnish into a paper cup, and add dabs of raw sienna, raw umber and lemon chrome oil colors to achieve a pale dirty brown. Thin down the varnish slightly with a little petroleum spirit.

18 Before painting the room, test the color of the varnish on a piece of white paper and on the painted walls. If the color is not right, wipe it off with a rag dipped in turps or petroleum spirit.

19 Using a soft ½-inch nylon brush, gently apply an even coat of the tinted varnish to all the walls, taking care not to dislodge the prints. As well as aging the room, the varnish will also help to seal the pictures onto the wall. Paint the door, door frame and baseboards with the same varnish. Leave to dry.

20 Apply a second coat the following day if necessary.

Floor

1 Find a piece of thick fabric which has a fairly neutral color. It should either be plain, or have a small pattern in the weave.

2 Cut the fabric to fit the room exactly. Stick the carpet onto the floor with fabric adhesive.

3 The baseboards can now be stuck to the walls with wood glue. They will help to keep the carpet down.

Assembling the Room

The furniture for this room is quite grand, and was bought from a doll house shop. The sofa and chairs have all been repainted, re-covered (see page 35), and trimmed with colored cord. Finishing touches include a leopardskin rug, (made in the same way as the tigerskin rug for the Scottish Baronial Hall, see page 25), vases of flowers, which are miniature dried flowers, and cushions, made from odd bits of fabric, painted by hand and trimmed with cord.

YELLOW DRAWING ROOM

The design of this room is inspired by a real room - Colefax and Fowler's Yellow Room. With its barrel-vaulted ceiling, deep, marbled moldings and double doors, it is a very grand, traditionally English drawing room. If you decide to copy or adapt the style of a real room, try to find a few photographs of the room, taken from different angles. Refer to these constantly while you are decorating and furnishing the room to get the details absolutely right.

Walls and Ceiling

1 To make the barrel-vaulted ceiling you need a length of polystyrene coving. Cut two strips to fit the depth of the room. Use a very sharp craft knife to cut the polystyrene - if you use a blunt knife the polystyrene will crumble and become messy. Again, using a very sharp scalpel, pare down the curves of coving that will be stuck to the ceiling so that, when they are in position, they form a smooth curve with the ceiling. The lower ends of the coving, which will be stuck to the wall, can be left since the cornice will go directly beneath them.

2 Stick the two lengths of coving onto the ceiling and walls with PVA adhesive. Then prime the outside of the coving with a 50:50 mixture of PVA and water.

3 When the coving is firmly in place smear some polyfilla onto the coving and ceiling with a palette knife and spread it out to give a smooth curve for the barrel-vaulted ceiling.

4 Apply white primer to the walls. Leave to dry. Pencil in the position of the double doors in the middle of the back wall.

5 Mix a slightly creamy white paint by tinting flat white oil paint with a tiny bit of raw umber. Draw a pencil line across the back wall at the height of the bottom of the polystyrene coving - this is where the cornice will be. Apply the paint to the ceiling, painting all the way across the barrel vault and on the back wall down to the pencil line. When it is dry, apply a second coat.

6 For the walls, mix a strong primrose-yellow paint, consisting of white semigloss tinted with lemon chrome and cadmium yellow oil colors. Apply an even coat of this paint to the walls with a small house paintbrush, but don't paint inside the penciled outline of the double doors on the back wall. Brush the paint out in all directions to avoid leaving brush marks in the paint. Leave to dry overnight. If little flashes of the white undercoat show through the yellow paint, apply a second coat.

Always mix enough paint for two coats - it is almost impossible to mix the same color a second time. Mix the paints in cup and, when you are not using them, cover the cup with plastic wrap. The paint will keep for quite a long time like this although it will develop a 'skin' on the top - you can pick this off and the paint underneath will be fine. If it is a bit thick, thin it with petroleum spirits or water.

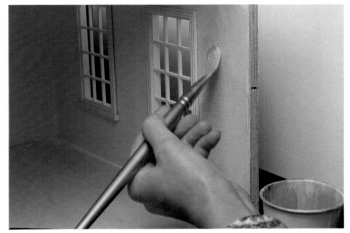

7 Mix a corn syrup-colored varnish by tinting clear gloss varnish with lemon chrome and raw sienna oil paints. Apply this to the yellow walls with a soft bristle or nylon brush, spreading the varnish thinly and evenly in all directions. This will make the color of the walls very strong and rich.

8 Paint the area inside the outline for the doors black.

9 Double doors can either be bought from a doll house shop or made in the same way as a normal door (see Victorian Nursery page 114). Apply a coat of white primer to the doors, and when that is dry apply a coat of white semigloss tinted with raw umber.

10 Pick out the moldings in the door frame, and the edges of the door panels in gold - use a fine-nibbed gold pen for this.

11 Stick the doors to the back wall with PVA.

12 The double doors are surrounded by mirrors - two long thin rectangular ones on either side, and a semicircular one above. Either get the mirrors cut to the correct size at a glass shop or, if you have a glass cutter, cut them yourself. Stick the mirrors around the door with PVA.

Floor

1 Cut out a piece of canvas to fit the room. Stain it with tea so that it is a dirty brown, and looks like matting.

2 Stick the canvas into the room with PVA around the edges.

Marbled Moldings

The moldings in this room are a cornice and a high baseboard. There is also a molded swag which will be hung on the back wall above the cornice. These are all marbled.

1 Cut lengths of cornice to fit the three walls.

2 The baseboards are very high, so you need to make these yourself. Cut lengths of hardwood which are approximately 1/8 inch thick and 1 1/4 inches high, and long enough to fit each wall. Then, cut three lengths of dado rail and stick them upside down on top of the hardwood with wood glue.

3 Apply a coat of white primer to all the pieces of cornice and baseboard. Leave to dry.

4 Apply two thick coats of white semigloss to all the cornices and baseboard so that the grain of the wood doesn't show through any more. Also, paint a piece of thin cardboard with a coat of white semigloss - this will be marbled and cut out in the shape of a swag to hang above the cornice. Leave to dry.

5 On a tin plate, make a very thin, watery glaze, consisting of flat white paint, watered down with petroleum spirit, and tinted with raw umber, and a little raw sienna and black to give a mousey gray-brown color. Test the color on a piece of baseboard and wipe it off quickly if it is not quite right. When you are satisfied with the color, apply a thin even coat to all the cornices and baseboards, and also to the piece of white cardboard. When you are painting the baseboards, leave the molding at the top white - if you get any paint on it by mistake, it can easily be wiped off with a cotton rag dabbed in petroleum spirit.

6 Take a pad of cotton rag and gently dab it onto all the painted moldings and the piece of cardboard to create a cloudy effect. Make sure that the rag gets right into all the moldings and returns of the cornice so the dark color doesn't build up in them, and keep turning the rag to vary the pattern.

7 Thin the paint mixture further with petroleum spirit. Dip a goose feather or turkey wing feather into the paint and, holding the feather lightly, fidget it across a piece of baseboard to get the basic marble pattern. Use both the side and tip of the feather, to vary the pattern. Keep the feather wet while you do this - if it dries too much, it will scratch the surface.

8 Vary the color of the paint by adding raw sienna, raw umber and black and start building up the veins in the marble. Try to emphasize existing patterns with stronger veins, and keep varying the color of the paint as you add more veins to create a really authentic marble look. The darker veins should be very fine; you will only need to use the tip of the feather for these.

9 Repeat this process on all the baseboards, cornices and the piece of cardboard. You will find the cornices more difficult because of all the molding. Force the feather across the ridges so that the veins look continuous - it may be easier to use a fine paintbrush to add the dark veins to the cornice. Leave to dry.

10 Apply clear semigloss varnish to all the marbled areas.

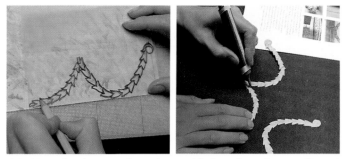

11 To make the swag from the marbled cardboard you will need to trace a swag from a photograph in a book or magazine. Transfer the tracing to the marbled cardboard and cut it with a very sharp scalpel. Then, with a dark gray or dark brown felt-tip pen add a bit more detail to the swags to make them more three-dimensional - so that each swag consists of sets of three leaves.

12 Stick the cornice onto the wall, directly below the coving, with PVA adhesive or double-sided tape.

13 Stick the marbled swag above the cornice on the back wall with PVA and stick the baseboard around the bottom of the walls with PVA or double-sided tape.

Making a Trefoil Pouf

1 Take three champagne corks and, using a craft knife, slice off the bottom of each cork so they are about 1¼ inches high.

2 Wind 1-inch wide double-sided tape around each cork and stick them together in a sort of triangle shape.

3 Cut out a piece of foam or padding to fit on top of the corks and secure it with some PVA. Cut out a rounded triangle of black velvet about ½ inch larger all round than the tops of the corks. Secure it with a little glue, taking care not to stretch it too tightly over the corks, as there will be a rosette in the center.

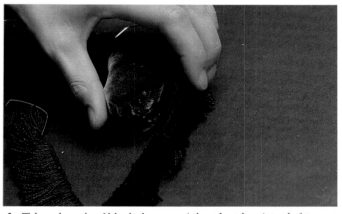

4 Take a length of black decorator's braid with a 1-inch fringe and wind it round the corks, sticking it to the double-sided tape, so that it forms a skirt round the pouf.

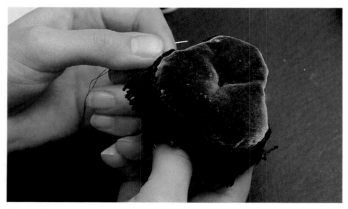

5 Make a rosette by knotting a piece of thread and winding the thread around the knot to make it larger. Sew a rosette onto the knot and stitch the rosette onto the velvet, thus pulling the fabric tightly across the top of the pouf. Secure the rosette by stitching through the bottom of one of the corks a few times.

Making a Mirror

The mirror above the fireplace is made from hardwood and moldings.

1   The mirror is approximately 2½ inches square, although this depends on the size of your room and your fireplace - the mirror should be the same width as the width of the fireplace. If you don't have a mirror that size, you can either get one cut at a glass shop, or you could cut it yourself if you have a glass cutter.

2   For the frame, cut lengths of wooden picture-frame molding, with mitered corners, to fit round the mirror; two strips of wood ⅛ inch thick and ½ inch wide to run down the sides, outside the molding; and one strip of wood ⅛ inch thick and ¾ inch wide to run along the top outside the moldings.

3   To make the pediment cut a strip of balsawood ⅛ inch thick, 1½ inches wide and about 1½ inches longer than the width of the mirror. Cut one strip of cornice molding, with mitered ends, to the same length as the balsawood. Cut two 1½ inch lengths of cornice molding. Miter one end of each strip at a 45 degree angle using a miter box, and cut the other end at a much more acute angle - about 30 degrees - so that they form the pediment when placed on top of the longer strip of cornice. You also need a small wooden urn to stick in the broken pediment.

4   Stick the three lengths of cornice onto the balsawood with the tops of the pediment touching the top edge of the balsawood, and the long strip of cornice about ½ inch above the bottom edge. Pencil in two curves from the tops of the pediment to the base of the pediment, and carefully cut along these curves, with a craft knife, to get a broken pediment.

5   Trim off the edges of balsawood around the top and sides of the pediment, and smooth any rough edges with sandpaper.

6   Take a piece of medium-weight white cardboard and assemble the frame on the cardboard, sticking the strips of wood onto the cardboard with PVA. Trim the card around the frame.

7   Apply white primer to the frame and the urn. When they are dry, apply a coat of white semigloss. Also, paint the fireplace with white semigloss. Leave to dry.

8   Stick the mirror inside the frame on the cardboard, with PVA.

9   Stick the fireplace into the room, with the mirror above it.

Reupholstering a Sofa

Doll house shops sell a wide range of furniture, some of which is very expensive, but they may not have exactly the right chair or sofa for a particular room. The best solution to this problem is to buy an inexpensive chair or sofa and reupholster it in the appropriate style. Use thin fabrics, such as silk, cotton or thin chintz, and try to avoid man-made fabrics because they don't hang well. If the fabric is patterned or striped, make sure that the pattern all runs in the same direction and the stripes join up.

1   Pull off the cushion, and the pieces of fabric on the front of the arms and the back of the sofa.

2   On a piece of tracing paper, draw the shapes of all the parts of the sofa that need to be recovered: the outside back, the inside back, two arms, the fronts of the arms, the cushion, and the front panel above the front legs. Make the shapes about ½ inch larger all round than the parts that they are covering. Also mark out one long strip to make a skirt which reaches the floor - this should be long enough to wind round the base of the sofa, with an extra 2 inches added to allow for the corner pleats.

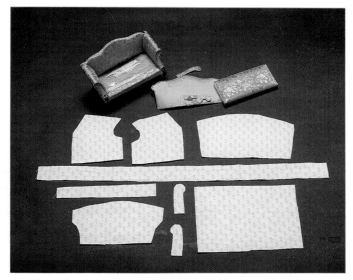

3   Place the templates on the fabric, making sure that the pattern on the fabric is all running in the same direction, and cut out the fabric around them with a pair of sharp scissors.

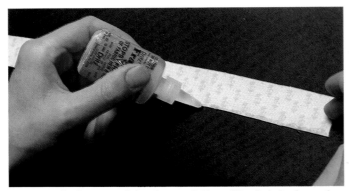

4 Treat the bottom of the skirt with Fray-Check (which can be bought from fabric shops or notions departments) to stop it fraying. If you don't have any Fray-Check you could hem it.

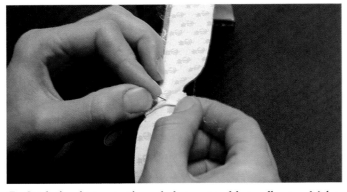

5 Stick the skirt onto the sofa first, using fabric adhesive. Make a ¹/₂-inch pleat at each corner, and pin the pleat to hold it in place until the glue is dry.

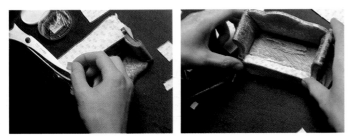

6 Next, stick the front panel above the skirt with fabric glue. Cut little nicks to make room for the arms of the sofa, fold over the top of the panel and secure it on the seat of the sofa.

7 Cover the arms, by wrapping the fabric over the arms and securing it with a little glue. You may need to cut little nicks in the fabric to make it fit tightly over the top of the arms. Fold the edges of the fabric round and stick onto the front of the arms.

8 Stick the fabric onto the inside back of the sofa. Again you might have to make little nicks in the fabric around the top of the arms so that it fits well.

9 Cover the cushion, the outside of the back, and the front of the arms and stick them in position.

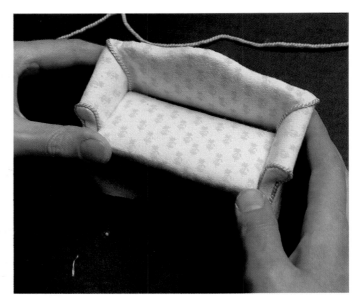

10 Finally, the sofa needs to be trimmed with braid or cord. The braid should match a color in the fabric - if you can't buy the right colored braid, dye white braid with watercolor inks or oil paints. Stick the braid along all the seams with fabric glue.

Making a Lamp

Lamp stands can be made from a variety of objects such as chunky beads, drapery-cord pulls, felt pens (for standard lamps) or you could even make them out of modeling clay - but whatever you use should have a hole through the middle.

1 The lamps for the Yellow Room are made from the handles for drapery cords. Cut off the bottom so they can stand up. Paint them with oil paints.

2 Make a wire frame from a piece of flower wire stuck into the hole at the top of the frame.

3 Slice a plastic bottle cap in half and wrap the tops of the wire around it to support it.

4 Make the lampshade by gathering a length of silk into pleats and making it into a circle. Place the shade over the support, and secure it with a couple of stitches if necessary.

Draperies

1 The draperies are made from very thin yellow silk or some similar fabric. Make a normal pair of drapes (see Scottish Baronial Hall, page 24), which are about an inch longer than they need to be to reach the floor.

2 Starting on the inside edge of each drape about two-thirds of the way up, sew a diagonal line of stitching to the top outside corner, and pull the stitching to gather the drapes upwards. Hem the bottom of the drape, sewing fishing weights into the hem to make the drapes hang well.

3 Cut three lengths of golden-colored upholstery cord (if you cannot buy the right color, dye white cord with watercolor inks or oil paints). Bind both ends of each length of cord with thread, sewn in and wound round several times 1/4 inch from the ends. Sew in a small curtain weight, and then fray the loose ends below it to make a tassel.

4 The first cord is draped into four equal swags or loops, each about 1 1/2 inches deep from the top of the drapes. The tasseled ends should hang down about two-thirds of the length of the drapes. The other two shorter lengths of cord are draped to form two smaller swags on each drape with tasseled ends hanging between the two drapes. Make five tiny trefoil bows from the same yellow fabric and sew them onto the drapes, covering the top of each swag.

5 Attach the drapes to a brass pole using seven loops of black cord instead of jewelry rings. The drapes are pulled by the diagonal stitched line rather than at the top.

6 Attach the brass curtain pole to the the cornice above the window. Hold a boiling kettle in the room for a few minutes to settle the gathers of the fabric.

Assembling the Room

While furnishing this room I have tried to copy the original room as closely as possible. The tables are all made by adapting the basic design for a table (see Charleston on page 119). The bookcases are also made by sticking strips of hardwood together with strips of molding at the top. The books in the bookcases can be bought from doll house shops, and painted in slightly faded colors. Alternatively, they can be made by cutting the stub end of an old cheque book into 1/2-inch lengths and painting them. The chandelier is made by making a frame from flower wire and threading clear beads onto the wire. Candle holders on the chandelier are sequins and the candles are tiny taper candles cut into short lengths. The large rug is a piece of cream-colored cotton velvet with a floral border which is drawn on with colored felt-tipped pens. The paintings are made by sticking a gilded frame around a postcard or a picture from an art catalog or magazine. Chinese vases, made from air-hardening modeling clay and painted, books and magazines are placed on the tables and the mantelpiece as well as large bowls and vases full of Fimo flowers.

The chandelier is made by threading beads onto a flower-wire frame.

The finished room, with its grand, but comfortable furnishings.

MANHATTAN LIVING ROOM

This 'Italian designer' living room is uncompromisingly modern. Pictures in magazines are a very useful source of inspiration when deciding how to decorate and furnish the room. The furniture is made from the most unlikely materials - black insulation foam and solder wire for the black leather sofa and chairs and wire champagne cages for the metal chairs. All the accessories and details are in keeping with the rather minimalist feel of the room.

Walls and Ceiling

1 Apply a coat of white primer to the walls, ceiling, door and window frames. When they are dry, sand them down lightly.

2 Mix a creamy yellow paint, consisting of white emulsion tinted with brilliant yellow. Apply to the walls and ceiling.

3 Paint the window frames black.

Floor

The large marble slabs of the floor are made by marbling a piece of lightweight cardboard, and then cutting it up into squares.

1 On a metal plate, mix a yellowy-beige glaze, consisting of white watercolor, diluted with plenty of water, and tinted with black, raw umber and brilliant yellow gouache or watercolors.

2 Make a puddle of diluted white watercolor on another plate, and put squeezes of black, raw umber, brilliant yellow and raw sienna on the edge of the plate. It is important to do these two steps before starting to paint, because watercolors dry in 10-15 minutes so you will need to work quite quickly.

3 Apply the glaze to a large piece of white cardboard quickly and roughly. (N.B. You will need this glaze again to paint the fireplace, so don't throw it away.)

4 Take a piece of cotton rag, fold it into a pad and gently dab the cardboard, taking paint off as you go. The ragging should be quite light, to achieve a cloudy pattern. Vary the direction of the rag so the pattern is not repeated.

5 Dip a feather in water and, using the broad end of the feather, cut through the paint on the card to make vague grainy marks.

6 Brush the cardboard with a badger brush to soften the grain.

7 Using the end of the feather, mix in some of the colors on the second plate, and fidget the feather across the cardboard to create the veins. Use the side of the feather as well as the tip to vary the width of the veins. Change the color of the paint each time you dip the feather in the paint to make darker and lighter veins. This will build up the texture of the marble. Leave to dry.

8 Apply two coats of oil-based gloss varnish to the cardboard.

Fireplace

1 Take a strip of balsawood or hardwood ⁵/₈ inch thick for the top and two verticals of the fireplace. The top is 1 inch wide and approximately 3 inches long - this will obviously depend on the width of the fireplace in your room. The uprights are ³/₄ inch wide and their height is equal to the height of the fireplace.

2 Using balsawood ¹/₈ inch thick, cut out two pieces to make the base of the fireplace. The first is a stubby T-shape to fit into the fire, and also to make the hearth. The second is simply a rectangle to fit into the fire on top of the base.

3 Stick the top of the fireplace onto the two uprights with wood glue. Stick the base parts together, also with wood glue.

4 Apply a coat of white primer to the fireplace and its base. Paint it on quite thickly so that the grain of the wood does not show. When it is dry, sand it down lightly.

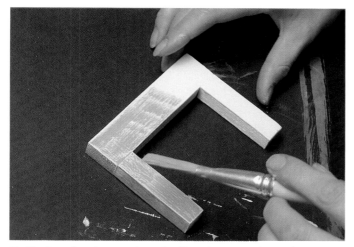

5 Darken the glaze used on the floor (see step 1) to achieve a sandy, stone color. Apply to the fireplace and its base quite roughly - don't worry if the brush marks show.

6 Dip your brush in the paint and, holding it over the fireplace, pull your finger through the bristles to spatter it with paint. Repeat the process several times, changing the color each time by adding dabs of white, raw umber, raw sienna, black, white and burnt umber, to build up the grainy texture of stone. Alter the consistency of the paint from time to time - this will change the size of the spots - the thinner the paint is, the larger the spots will be. Leave to dry. Apply two coats of oil-based gloss varnish to the fireplace and leave to dry.

7 Stick the fireplace into position with PVA adhesive.

8 Cut the marbled cardboard into 2-inch squares.

9 Stick the marble slabs into the room with PVA, trimming them where necessary to fit around the fireplace and door.

Making a Black Leather Chair

1 The black leather chairs are made from black self-adhesive insulation foam and solid solder. For the arms of each chair, cut strips of insulation foam 4$\frac{1}{4}$ inches long and 2$\frac{1}{4}$ inches wide, using a craft knife. For the back cut a strip of foam 4$\frac{1}{4}$ inches long and 2 inches wide; for the seat cut a strip 3$\frac{1}{2}$ inches long and 2 inches wide; and for the cushion a strip 1$\frac{3}{4}$ inch long and 2 inches wide.

2 For the chair legs, cut four lengths of solid solder 1¼ inches long with a pair of pliers. With a felt-tipped pen, make a mark on the solder ½ inch from one end - this indicates where the leg is positioned when the foam is stuck together.

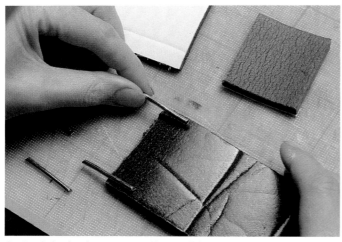

3 Peel the backing paper off one of the arm pieces of foam. Position the two lengths of solder wire ⅛ inch in from the edges of the foam, with the ½-inch mark on the bottom of the piece of foam (so that ¾ inch is sticking out).

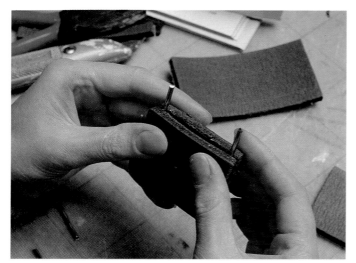

4 Fold the foam in half so that it sticks together, holding the legs securely in place. The adhesive backing is very strong, so make sure that you stick it in exactly the right place - it is almost impossible to peel it apart and re-stick it if you make a mistake. Repeat the process with the other arm.

5 Peel off the backing from the back the chair, and fold it in half so it sticks together. Repeat on the seat of the chair.

6 Stick the seat of the chair onto the back with PVA adhesive.

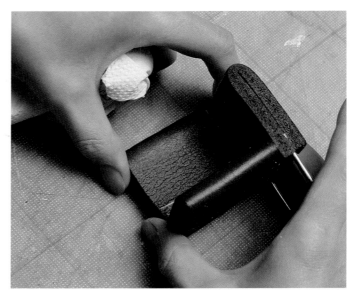

7 Now stick the arms of the chair onto the seat and back.

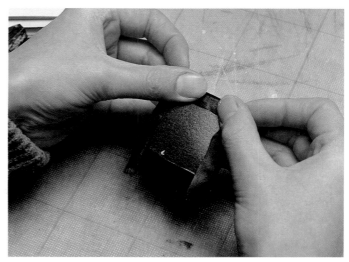

8 Cover the cushion with black nylon or some other shiny fabric. Cut the fabric so that it is ½ inch larger than the cushion all the way round. Peel off the backing of the foam, and fold the fabric over the cushion so that it sticks onto the back. Finally, place the cushion in the chair.

9 Dilute a little PVA with water. Using a bristle brush, apply a coat of the PVA to the front and back edges of the arms of the chair. This will act as a varnish and make them much shinier.

Making a Black Leather Sofa

1 To make a black leather sofa, cut strips of insulation foam the same size as for the chair (see step 1 above). You will need two strips each for the back, seat and cushion of the sofa.

2 Peel off the backing of the strips of foam and fold them in half to make the arms, back and seat of the sofa.

3 Cut a length of solid solder approximately 16 inches long.

4 Bend the solid solder to form the front legs, tops of the arms and back of the sofa. Use a pair of pliers to bend the solder into curved right angles. The legs are 3 inches high, the tops of the arms are 2¼ inches and the back is 4 inches. Trim the legs if necessary so that they are the same height.

5 Cut two pieces of solder 3 inches long for the back legs.

6 Cut two 4-inch lengths of solder for the seat supports.

7 Cut two pieces of solder and bend them into shape so that they run from one front leg, around the back of the sofa, to the other front leg. These will support the back of the sofa.

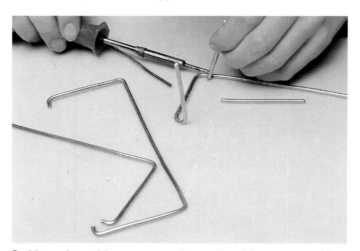

8 Using thin solder containing flux and a soldering iron, solder the two back legs to the back of the frame, just inside the corners. You might find that you need someone to help with this as there is a lot to hold at once.

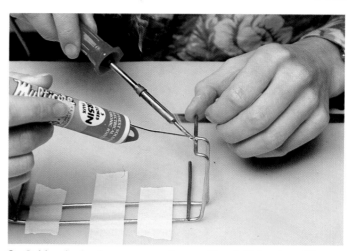

9 Solder the back supports to the outside of all four legs. This is quite fiddly so you might find it easier to stick the frame and back supports to your cutting board with masking tape to keep them in position while you do this.

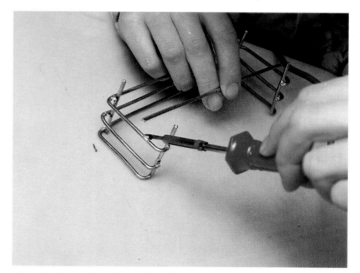

10 Finally, solder the ends of the two seat supports to the sides of the bottom back support.

11 Cover the cushions with a shiny black fabric such as nylon.

12 Varnish the ends of the arms with diluted PVA.

13 Place the arms, seats, backs and cushions of the sofa into the frame. They should fit quite tightly, and will support themselves within the frame.

Making Chairs from Wire Champagne Cork Cages

1 To make each chair you will need two wire cork cages from champagne bottles and thin solder containing flux. The first cage will form the legs and seat of the chair. Cut the circular wire at the bottom with pliers, and pull it off. You will be left with the four verticals, which become the legs of the chair, and the metal top which is the seat.

2 To make the back of the chair, pull out the metal cap from the second wire cage. Cut the top and bottom circles and remove two of the vertical pieces of wire. Bend the loose horizontal wires diagonally across and wind them round the opposite corners. Trim any loose ends of wire and solder them to hold them in position.

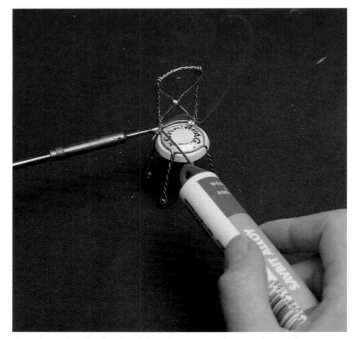

3 Then, fix the back of the chair onto the seat by soldering the two pieces together.

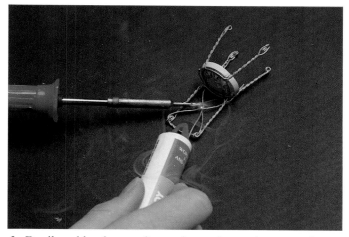

4 Finally, solder the two diagonals together at the point where they cross in the middle of the back.

Blinds

The slats of the Venetian blinds are made from narrow strips of thin hardwood (from model or hobby shops) and are joined by sewing them together with colorless nylon thread, with a bead between each slat.

1 Cut the strips so that they are the same length as the width of the window. Make pencil marks ¹/₂ inch from both ends of each strip of hardwood - these are the positions through which the needle and thread will pass.

2 Thread a very fine-pointed beading needle with colorless nylon thread. Knot the end of the thread and stick the needle through the first slat on the pencil mark. Then thread it through a small bead, and then the next slat. Continue until the blind is long enough to hang halfway down the window.

3 Sew three more slats onto the blind, without any beads between them. This will give the impression of the bottom of the blind being bunched up.

4 Now secure the thread on the final slat by overcasting it.

5 Repeat the process on the other end of the blind.

6 Cut a strip of slightly thicker hardwood to the size of the slats of the blind. Stick this thicker strip to the top slat of the blind with wood glue. This will act as a support for the blind.

7 Attach the top of the blind to the inside of the window frame with double-sided adhesive pads.

Assembling the Room

Place the furniture in the room. Glass-topped tables are made by getting plain or smoked glass cut to size and shape at a hobby shop or builders store. The tables can be supported by a solid solder frame, or by finding a cylinder of metal or smoked acrylic and attaching it to the table as a single column. The glass ball sculpture is made by making a block of wood by sticking chunks of balsawood together, priming it and marbling it with white, gray and black watercolors - make sure that the veins go round the corners of the cube to give the impression of a solid block of marble. Then, apply two coats of semigloss varnish and attach the glass ball with Grip Wax (from doll house shops). Furnish the room with hi-tech electrics - television and speakers. Miniature televisions can be bought in toy stores and painted black, and speakers made by painting blocks of wood the appropriate colors. Modern paintings can be made by sticking illustrations from art magazines onto pieces of hardwood. Finishing touches include a vase of lilies, made from Fimo, and miniature magazines on the tables.

AN EDWARDIAN TOWN HOUSE

When deciding how to decorate the exterior of a doll house, it is well worth consulting a few books on architecture or even scanning the streets themselves. But, most important of all, you should consider the existing structural features. This Edwardian house, for example, is edged by corner-stones or quoins and I have used these as a guide for determining the size of the honey-colored stones. This style is in keeping with real houses of this age and type.

Preparation

1 Apply a coat of matt white paint to all the outer surfaces of the house except for the roof. On the roof, apply an undercoat of primer which has been tinted a pale mauve with a little crimson and a little ultramarine. Using a small brush, apply a coat of white semigloss to the doors and windows.

2 Leave to dry overnight. Then, smooth the surface of the house lightly and evenly with sandpaper. The surface is now ready for applying the glaze.

The Stonework

1 Take a pencil and mark the edges of the stones on the façade. You will find that the matt white undercoat will absorb the pencil marks better than a semigloss undercoat would have done. Since the pencil lines should show through the glaze which you will apply later, use a hard pencil whose marks will not be washed away. I have made the stones ³/4 inch high - the same height as the corner-stones - and 1¹/4 inches wide; this is equivalent to stones on a real house which are 9 inches high and 15 inches wide. But vary the widths slightly and stagger them, just as a builder would lay the stones. For example, don't end a stone too near to a window. If you make a mistake, simply rub it away with an eraser.

2 Mix a warm yellow, sandstone-colored glaze, consisting of matt white paint tinted with raw sienna, cadmium yellow and a dash of raw umber and thin it down with a little white spirit. Apply it to the surface of the house with a soft bristle brush, avoiding the woodwork. A hard brush would scratch away the pencil marks which you want to show through. Paint one side at a time and then rag it before it dries.

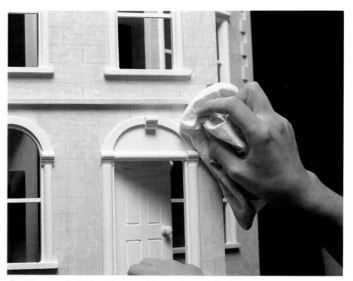

3 To rag, dab the glaze softly with a pad of cotton rag to create a gently textured background that will give the impression of variations in the stone colour. Don't worry if a few of the pencil lines merge into the paint; this will give them more interest.

The Slate Roof

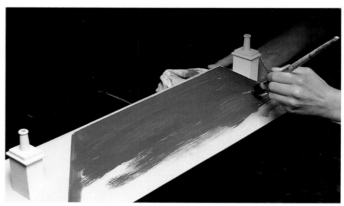

1 For the slate roof, mix a gray glaze, consisting of a tiny speck of matt white with equal quantities of crimson, ultramarine and black. Thin the glaze to the consistency of milk with petroleum spirit. Apply this quickly and evenly to one side of the roof.

2 When it is covered, take an old 1-inch house paintbrush and pull it back through the glaze along the roof. This technique, in which the bristles rearrange the paint in fine straight lines and expose streaks of the undercoat is known as dragging.

3 Then, fold a rag between your thumb and forefinger and lightly rub the paint away from the ridge and edges of the roof. This will lighten those areas. Repeat these three steps on the other side of the roof. Leave to dry overnight.

Front Door

On the front door, apply two coats of blue gloss or semigloss.

Chimney Stacks

1 Apply the honey-colored glaze to the bases of the chimneys.

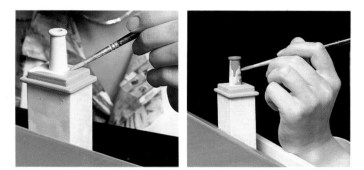

2 Mix a paler gray glaze for the bottom of the chimney pots, consisting of matt white paint and a little of the original slate mixture plus some raw umber. Apply this with a sable brush. You might like to paint the front doorstep in the same color too. For the brick chimney pots themselves, you need only a tiny amount of paint. Mix some burnt sienna with a little matt white and a dash of cadmium scarlet and black. (Experiment until you are happy with the color.) Then apply it neatly with a sable brush. Finally, paint the inside of the chimney pots black.

COUNTRY KITCHEN

This is a very traditional country kitchen with oak-beamed walls and ceiling. It is furnished with a large oak table and chairs, a dresser and an old range. In a cluttered room like this it is important that all the accessories and details are in keeping with the character of the room - baskets of fresh vegetables, dishtowels hanging over chairs, lots of china on the dresser, a wooden plate rack on the wall and even some washing-up in the sink are all appropriate to this kitchen.

Walls and Ceiling

1 Apply a coat of white primer to the walls and ceiling.

2 Next, make beams for the walls and ceiling from hardwood. Try to buy wood with a fairly straight grain - if the grain is too wavy, it will not look so good when it is cut into such thin strips.

3 The beams for walls are made from hardwood 1/16 inch thick (if you cannot get this, use balsawood). Break the wood into strips rather than cut it, so that the beams are not all the same width and have a rough, rustic look. Trim the ends so that the length of the strips is the same as the height of the room.

4 The ceiling beams are made from hardwood strips 1/8 inch thick and 3/8 inch wide. Cut the strips into lengths that fit across the ceiling from one side to the other.

5 There will also be horizontal beams at the top of each wall - almost like a cornice. Those on the side walls are 1/8 inch thick and 1/4 inch wide and the one across the back wall is 1/8 inch thick and 3/8 inch wide. Trim the lengths to fit the walls.

6 The baseboards are strips of hardwood 1/8 inch thick, 3/8 inch wide and long enough to fit the walls. Do not miter the corners - they want to look really rustic.

7 Cut strips of hardwood to fit around the window. These will be stuck on top of the existing window frame.

8 Next, stain all the beams with a dark oak wood stain. I used a mixture of Georgian medium oak and Jacobean dark oak. Dab a bit of each onto a rag and rub it into the strips of wood. Keep the rag quite damp with the stain and rub it in hard. Make sure that you stain the edges of the beams as well as the side that will be showing. Mixing the different-colored stains on the rag will give slightly different oaky colors each time you add more - this will make the beams look more authentic when they are all in place. Leave to dry for at least six hours or overnight if possible.

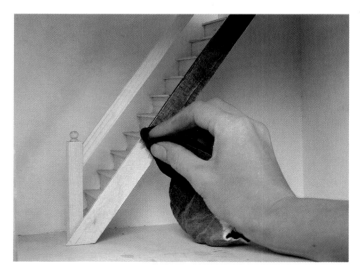

9 Stain the staircase and banisters with the same wood stains. It is a good idea to stick masking tape around the ceiling and walls at the top of the stairs, so you don't stain them as well.

10 When the stain on the beams is dry, spray a layer of semi-gloss polyurethane varnish onto all the beams.

11 Check that all the beams fit into the room - you will need to cut the beams for the back wall to fit around the staircase. It is a good idea to keep the two parts of the beams that have been cut together with a bit of masking tape. This will avoid any muddle later when you are sticking them onto the wall.

12 To give the walls a rough plastery look, mix white matt emulsion with a similar quantity of fine surface plaster filler (you can use ready-mixed plaster filler or powder). Use an old house paintbrush for this, as the plaster filler is rather harsh on brushes. The beams will stick to this and sink into it to look more realistic. Add water until it has a thick creamy consistency, and make sure that it is really well mixed.

13 Tint the paint-filler mixture with brilliant yellow, raw umber and burnt sienna gouache to achieve a good old-looking creamy color. Test it on the wall, and hold a beam against it to make sure it looks right. If it doesn't, you can wipe it off with a rag, and adjust the color. Finally mix in a teaspoon of PVA adhesive, to ensure that the beams stick to the wall really well.

14 Paint this mixture onto the back wall - apply it thickly and roughly so that the brush marks are visible. Stick the beams onto the back wall, about 1-1½ inches apart, pressing them into the paint. The beams above and below the staircase should line up with each other. The spaces between the beams need not be too exact - a slight randomness looks more realistic.

15 Next, paint the mixture onto the ceiling, and stick the beams across the ceiling (i.e. from left to right), again about 1-1½ inches apart. You will find that you have to work quite quickly; the paint dries in about ten minutes, so you must get all the beams stuck onto the ceiling or wall in that time.

16 Then, paint the side walls, one at a time, and stick the beams down - position the beams on the walls so that they join up with the beams on the ceiling.

17 Stick the three horizontal wall beams across the top of each wall with PVA adhesive. These will add extra support to the vertical beams on the walls.

18 Finally, stick the four short strips of stained and varnished hardwood onto the existing window frame, with PVA adhesive - this will give it the same rustic feel as the rest of the room.

Floor

The rush matting for the floor is made out of an old beach mat - but you could use a very thinly woven table mat.

1 Stain the matting with strong tea. You will probably need about four teabags in a mug of boiling water. When it is quite cool, simply paint the tea generously onto both sides of the matting so that it really soaks right into the straw. This gives it a slightly old, dirty look. Leave the matting to dry. If it is still too pale, paint on some more tea.

2 Make a template of the floor with a piece of newspaper, taking care to cut accurately around the staircase. Cut the matting out around the template so that it fits into the room, and around the stairs. To stop it fraying, stick double-sided tape around all the edges; fold the fraying bits over and stick them onto the back of the double-sided tape.

3 Stick the matting down with PVA or double-sided tape.

4 Stick the baseboards onto the walls with wood glue.

Assembling the Room

The curtains are made from a scrap of fabric, cut and hemmed to fit the window. The curtain pole is threaded through the top hems of the curtains, and nailed to the wall above the window frame. The table and chairs have been distressed to make them look older. The dresser and draining board are made from hardwood, and the sink is made from air-drying modeling clay (see Modern Kitchen, page 55). The kitchen should look very 'lived in', so there is lots of china on the dresser, pots and pans lying around, and bowls of fruit, and other food on the table and dresser (see page 60 for making food).

MODERN KITCHEN

The idea here is to create a thoroughly modern, hi-tech kitchen. Catalogs from kitchen shops are very good sources of inspiration. The main features are a series of white fitted base and wall units and an island in the middle of the room with a large ventilator fan above it. The simplicity of the design and the clean, uncluttered surfaces make this a totally functional room which is in complete contrast to the Country Kitchen.

Walls and Ceiling

1 Apply a coat of white primer to the ceiling and any walls that will not be covered with units or tiles. Leave to dry.

2 Apply a coat of flat white emulsion to the ceiling and the walls that have been primed.

Floor

1 Take a piece of thin cork and apply two thick coats of PVA - this acts as a varnish and will make the cork darker and very shiny. Leave to dry.

2 Cut the cork so that it fits exactly into the room, and stick it to the floor with PVA.

Making Kitchen Units

All the units are made to the same basic design, with slightly different features. They are made from styrene plastic sheets (from model shops). The best thicknesses of sheet styrene to use are 0.030 or 0.040 - these are thick enough to be quite sturdy and thin enough to cut with a craft knife. You will need plenty of sheets of styrene plastic. Before starting work on the units, draw an exact plan of the room and work out the sizes and positions of the units on the plan. A good size for the base units are 2 inches wide, 2 inches deep and 3 inches high. The wall units are 2 inches wide, 1 inch deep, and high enough to reach the ceiling when they are stuck to the wall 2 inches above the top of the base units. It is important to be accurate with the measurements at this stage, otherwise the units will not fit exactly into the kitchen.

1 Mark and cut out the styrene into the panels for the back, sides, base and door for each unit. When cutting styrene, it is best to lightly score the line with a craft knife, and then score the same line once or twice more and then break the styrene - it will break cleanly along the line. There is no need to make a top, because a work surface will be made later to cover all the units.

2 If you are making a base unit, cut out a little rectangle from the bottom of the side panels 1/2 inch high and 1/8 inch deep - this is where the baseboard is set back. Cut a strip of styrene 1/2 inch wide for the baseboard. Paint it black.

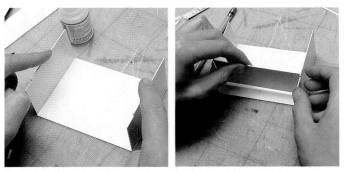

3 Stick the sides of the unit to the back with super glue. Hold the pieces of styrene together for about a minute while the glue sets. Stick the base immediately above the baseboard ledge.

4 The handles on the doors of cupboards are staples from a staple gun. Position the staple gun so that the staple will be at the top of the door. Put something very hard (a miter box for example) behind the styrene so that the staple doesn't go right through. Punch the staple into the door - it should go halfway in. If it is a bit bent, straighten it out with a pair of pliers.

5 Stick the door onto the cupboard with double-sided tape down one side to act as a hinge.

6 A double unit can be made in the same way by following steps 1-5 above, but making the back, base and baseboard twice as wide, and making two doors.

7 This basic design can be varied to make a range of different units. An oven can be made in the same way but the door is made by sticking a piece of black tulle or gauze between two sheets of clear acetate with a tiny bit of PVA around the edges. Trim the edges of the door with silver-colored Scotch tape and make the dials of the oven from sequins.

8 A dishwasher is made in the same way as the basic unit, but the door is attached at the bottom, so that it opens downwards. The control panel is made by sticking silver Scotch tape across the top of the unit, and gluing sequins onto it.

9 Some units may have drawers instead of cupboards. If so, mark the drawers on the front panel with a pencil, and staple handles into the middle of each drawer.

10 The microwave oven is 1 inch high, 2 inches wide and 1 inch deep. Cut a strip off one side of the front panel ¼ inch wide. Paint this black, stick sequins onto it for dials, and stick it to the front of the microwave with superglue. To make the door, cut a rectangular hole in the other part of the front panel. Stick two pieces of acetate, with black tulle or gauze sandwiched between them, behind the hole. Attach the door to the microwave with double-sided tape.

Next, make the counter tops to cover the base units. One will be a simple surface, and one will contain the sinks (see below). Remember that one of these will have to be about 2 inches longer than the row of units so that it goes into the corner of the room.

11 To make the simple counter top, cut a piece of balsawood ³/₃₂ inch thick to cover the row of units - it should be slightly deeper than the units. Cut a sheet of styrene plastic exactly the same size as the balsawood and stick them together with superglue. Trim the edges of the work surface that will not be against the wall with a strip of silver Scotch tape along the edge, so that about ⅛ inch of the Scotch tape is on the top.

Making an Island Unit

1 The island in the center of the room is a double unit, containing drawers and cupboards. Make a counter top for the island in the same way as for the base units (see step 11 below). Trim the edges with silver Scotch tape and stick the top onto the island with PVA adhesive.

2 The range is made from a piece of styrene plastic, painted black, and varnished to make it shiny. Cut the styrene to the right size, and stick four very small keyrings or jewelry rings onto the card with PVA and stick sequins onto the edge for dials. Trim the edges with silver tape and stick it onto the top with PVA.

3 The ventilator fan which hangs from the ceiling above the range is made from a piece of lightweight silver cardboard and the top of a lipstick holder, or some similar cylindrical object. Cover the lipstick top with aluminium foil.

4 Then cut the silver cardboard into a rectangle approximately 4 inches by 3 inches. Bend the rectangle into a semicircular dome. Cut two semicircles from the cardboard to fit the ends of the dome and stick them into position. Cut a hole in the top of the curve and stick the lipstick top into it, securing it with PVA.

5 Make a bar to hang below the front of the ventilator fan from a piece of thin solder. Bend the ends of the wire and secure them to the inside of the ventilator fan with Scotch tape.

Making the Kitchen Sink

The kitchen sink fits into the top of one of the units. I have decided to make two circular sinks to fit into the top of a double cupboard unit.

1 To make each sink you will need some air-dry modeling clay and a large bottle cap or small pot which is the right size. Air-dry clay needs to be kept damp and cool; it sets when it is left to dry. Mold the modeling clay around the pot and trim off any excess; damp the edges of the clay and mold them into a smooth join. Leave to dry for 24 hours. It is a good idea to take the pot out of the modeling clay after about 6-8 hours.

2 The modeling clay will be white when it is completely dry. Paint a small black circle in the bottom of the sink for the plug hole. To make the sink look more like porcelain, apply a coat of clear gloss varnish to give it a good shine.

3 To make the counter top for the row of units that includes the sink unit, cut a piece of balsawood to fit the row of units - again make the balsawood slightly deeper than the base units.

4 The metal rims of the sinks are made from the rims of small tea strainers. Remove the mesh from the rims of the strainers. Place the rims on the balsawood in the correct positions for the sinks and, with a pencil, draw around the inside of the rims.

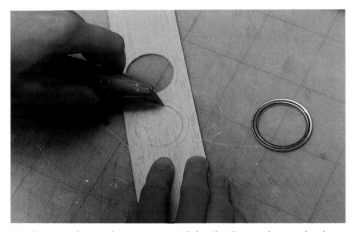

5 Cut out the circles, using a craft knife. Cut each one slowly and carefully, scoring a little bit at a time. It is a good idea to cut slightly inside the penciled circle - you can always sand it down to the right size later. Smooth any rough edges with sandpaper.

6 Cut a piece of styrene exactly the same size as the balsawood. Mark the two circles for the sink on the styrene and cut them out with a craft knife. Stick the styrene and the balsawood together with super glue. Trim the front edges with silver tape.

7 Stick the metal rims around the holes on the work surface with super glue. Make a tiny hole between the two sinks at the back of the counter top for the tap. The tap is made by sticking one half of a screw-together jewelry clasp into the hole in the styrene, and sticking half a paper clip into that.

8 Make a balsawood shelf and stick it into the sink unit with super glue so that the sinks reach the counter top when they are sitting on the shelf.

9 When the superglue has set firmly, place the bowls on the shelf and stick them in position so that they are directly beneath the holes in the counter top.

Assembling the Room

1 When you have made all the units, stick the base units into the room with super glue or PVA. Stick the baseboard, which has been painted with black oil colors, onto the bottom of the base units. Stick the counter tops onto the units with super glue.

2 Make pencil marks on the wall to indicate the positions of the wall units - remember they will reach the ceiling.

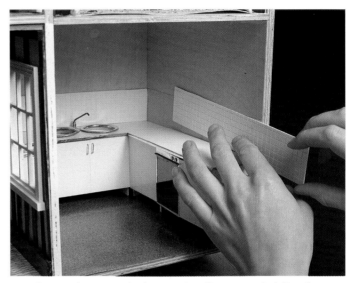

3 The area between the base and wall units is tiled. Ready-made sheets of tiles can be bought from model shops - use sheets with 1/4-inch square tiles (this is equivalent to 3-inch tiles in a real kitchen). Cut the sheets of tiles to fit between the two sets of units and stick them to the walls with super glue or PVA.

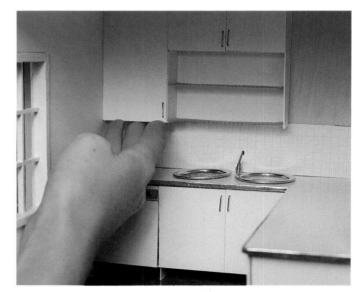

4 Stick the wall units onto the wall with super glue or PVA.

5 Place the island in the center of the room, and secure the ventilator fan to the ceiling with super glue or PVA.

This kitchen is totally functional, so don't clutter it up too much. The window shade is made by winding some fabric around a piece of dowel and is attached to the wall above the window frame. The stool is a door stopper - the pad is covered with black silk. Finally, hang miniature ladles, made from jewelry findings and solder, and other kitchen utensils from the extractor fan and place pots and pans on the surfaces and on the shelves.

COLONIAL DINING ROOM

This dining room is almost puritanical in character, with simple wooden furnishings and one naive picture above the mantelpiece. The colors are muted and earthy - brick-red, green and mustard, which is picked up in the formal drapes. The only decorative objects are the orange trees and a few things on the mantelpiece. Today, however, is Thanksgiving, so the table has been set with the best silverware and pewter plates, starched white linen napkins and six candles. A feast has been prepared - pumpkin soup, then turkey and cranberry sauce with pumpkin pie to finish.

Floor

1 Make oak planks from balsawood, and paint on graining (see Scandinavian Bedroom, page 70)

2 Darken and 'polish' the planks by applying a coat of varnish tinted with raw umber. Leave to dry.

3 Lay the planks across the room from side to side, and stick them onto the floor with PVA.

Walls

1 Apply white primer to the walls and ceiling. When they are dry, lightly sand down the surfaces.

2 Mix a creamy-off white paint by adding small quantities of raw umber, raw sienna and a tiny bit of black gouache to white distemper (or matt-finish white emulsion if you don't have distemper). Apply a coat of this paint to the walls. Leave to dry.

3 Add a little more white to the paint mixture to make it lighter, and apply a coat of this lighter paint to the ceiling.

4 Cut lengths of baseboards, cornice and dado to fit each wall. Miter the ends and apply a coat of primer. Leave to dry.

5 On a plate, mix a mustard-colored paint, consisting of white emulsion tinted with dabs of yellow ochre, raw sienna, raw umber and a dash of black and olive green gouache. Using a flat hog's hair brush apply a coat of this emulsion to the baseboards, door frame, mantelpiece, and window frames.

6 Mix a creamy off-white paint by tinting white emulsion with raw umber and raw sienna. Apply to the dado, door and cornice.

Stenciling the Walls

1 Pictures of stenciled walls can be found in magazines and books. Photocopy and reduce the stencils so that they are the right size for your room. Trace the reduced stencils onto tracing paper. I used two different patterns, which will alternate around the room. The first is a geometric pattern and the second is of flowers and leaves. For this, you need one stencil for the flowers and another for the leaves as they are painted different colors.

2 Transfer each tracing onto a separate strip of stenciling paper. This can be bought, or made by applying a coat of acrylic gloss medium and varnish to both sides of a sheet of construction paper to make it waterproof. Repeat each pattern several times so that a whole line of stencils can be transferred in one go.

3 If you are using more than one stencil to make one pattern (e.g. flowers and leaves above), cut small registration holes at the top of each strip of stencil paper - this will ensure that the stencils line up as the different parts are added.

4 Using a sharp scalpel with a fine-pointed blade, cut out the stencilled shapes. This can be quite tricky, and requires a lot of patience. Generally, when cutting curves it is easier to cut towards yourself - but be very careful, and work slowly.

5 Mix a slightly faded olive-green paint, consisting of white distemper or emulsion (whichever you used for the walls) tinted with olive green and raw umber. This is for the leaves, and also for the geometric pattern. Also, mix a soft brick-red paint by tinting white distemper or emulsion with burnt sienna and cadmium red - this is for the flowers. Test both colors with the stencil sheets on a piece of white paper.

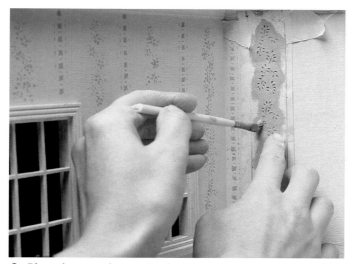

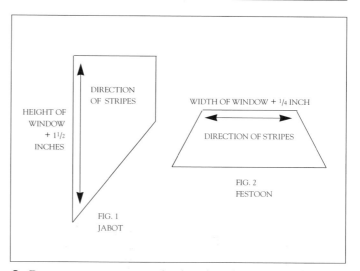

6 Place the stencil paper for the leaves at the edge of one of the side walls, mark the registration holes and secure it with masking tape. If, however, a wall has two windows, or a central feature, stick the first stencil in the middle and work out from there. Using a stiff bristle brush, gently dab the paint through the holes. It is important not to have too much paint on the brush, because it will just dribble and become blobby and messy.

7 Stick the stencil for the geometric pattern to the wall, so that it is about 1 inch from the leaf pattern. Again, gently paint through the holes with the green paint.

8 Repeat steps 6 and 7 around each wall at intervals of about 1 inch. Leave to dry. If you make a mess, you can rub the paint off quickly with a damp rag. It is also a good idea to keep the paint that was used on the walls, to touch up any untidy patches.

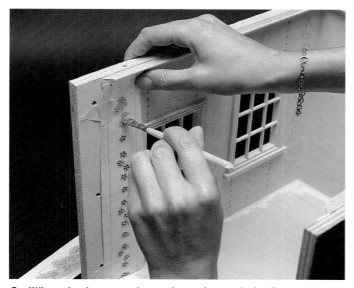

9 When the first sets of stencils are dry, stick the flower stencil in position, making sure that the registration holes are in the same position as they were for the leaves. Paint through the holes with the brick-red paint. Leave to dry.

Draperies

The draperies in this room are known as festoons (or swags) and jabots (the drapes). They are purely decorative, since they do not pull.

1 The fabric for the drapes is mustard-colored cotton, with a thin, darker mustard stripe. For each window you will need to cut out two jabots and one festoon.

2 Draw out a paper pattern for the jabots (see fig 1. for shape). The long vertical should be 1½ inches longer than the height of the window (including the frame). The width should be 2 inches wider than the width of the window (including frame). Place the pattern on the fabric and cut out the jabots. Make sure that the verticals of the pattern run along the stripes of the fabric.

3 Iron fabric stiffener or fusable interfacing onto the back of each piece of fabric.

4 Hem the long vertical edge, or iron on fabric interlining which sticks the hem down. Iron-on tape is better as it doesn't show, and the fabric lies much flatter than if it was hemmed.

5 Trim the diagonal of each jabot by sewing mustard-colored picot braid onto the edge of the fabric. Continue sewing the braid until it is about half way up the shorter vertical.

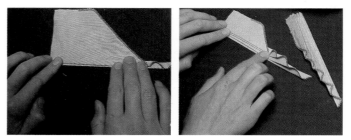

6 Start folding the fabric to make five pleats in the jabot. Each pleat is about ¼ inch wide, and should be folded so that it does not overlap the previous one. If the pleats don't look quite even, you can rearrange them to make them the same size.

7 Secure the pleats with a few stitches at the top. Press with a medium-hot iron to flatten the pleats and hold them in position.

8 Draw and cut out out the shape of the festoon on a piece of paper (see fig. 2 for shape). The shorter edge should be ¹/₄ inch wider than the width of the window, including the frame.

9 Place the paper pattern on the fabric, with the parallel sides of the pattern running along the stripes of the fabric, and cut out one festoon for each window. Trim the longer of the two horizontal edges with mustard-colored picot braid.

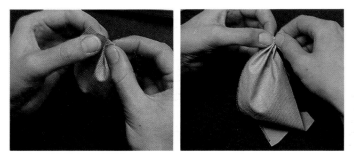

10 Holding the braided edge of the festoon, gather the fabric, making about five pleats, towards the opposite edge. Pin the pleats to secure them. Gather the opposite side in the same way. Arrange the festoon so that the pleats fan out as they hang down in the middle, and stitch both ends to secure the pleats.

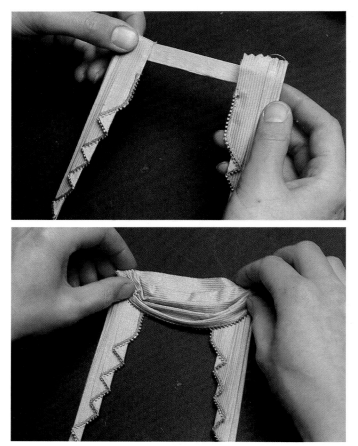

11 Cut a narrow strip of thin hardwood, approximately ¹/₄ inch longer than the width of the window frame. Place the jabots at either end of this, with the end pleat tucked behind the wood. Stick them onto the wood with fabric adhesive. Stick the festoon onto the wood, folding the top pleat behind the wood.

12 Stick the wooden strip to the wall, above the window frame, with PVA adhesive.

Making Food

Making miniature food for doll house rooms is not only great fun; it also adds a perfect finishing touch to any kitchen or dining room in a house. The basic ingredient for all doll house food is Fimo. This is a modeling material. It comes in a number of different colors, but it is more economical to use white Fimo and paint it. It is best to start by making simple things like eggs, potatoes, carrots, peas, bacon and then move on to more difficult shapes, such as turkeys and ham. Whatever you are making use the same basic method:

1 Break off a bit of Fimo and soften it up in your hand and mold it into whatever shape you require.

2 Bake the Fimo food in the oven at a low temperature for about 15-20 minutes.

3 Paint with oil colors when cool, adding a little varnish to the paint if you want the food to be shiny. There are, however, a few variations on this method:

Making a Quiche

1 Use a bottle cap for the shape of the quiche base. Line it with aluminium foil and mold the Fimo into the top.

2 Bake the quiche base inside the bottle cap for 7 minutes.

3 Take the base out of the bottle cap and return it to the oven for a further 8-10 minutes. If you bake the Fimo in the bottle cap for too long, you won't be able to remove it.

4 Fill the quiche bases with a mixture of varnish and tapioca, to create a textured filling.

Onions

1 Mold the Fimo until it is soft.

2 Wrap it round a thin strip of raffia.

3 Wrap a piece of dampened real onion skin or shallot skin around the Fimo and bake in the oven for 10-15 minutes.

Bread

Miniature bread can be made from real bread dough to make it look more realistic and floury. Put plenty of salt in the dough to keep the mice away. Before baking in the oven, you could work little pieces of tea leaf into the dough to look like currants. You can also make bread from Fimo by following the basic Fimo recipe.

Mincemeat Tarts

1 Cut out a small circle of Fimo, and stick it onto a sequin. This will help hold its shape.

2 Make a slight dent in the Fimo with the end of a pencil, so that the pie can be filled.

3 Bake in the oven.

4 Fill the tart with varnish mixed with tea leaves.

Use varnish as a medium when making food. All sorts of colored paints and ingredients, such as tea leaves, dried flowers and tapioca, can be added to create a range of different textures and colors.

Making Candle Sconces

1 The sconces are made from bottle caps. Using a pair of pliers, flatten the crimping outwards all round the bottle cap.

2 Soak the top in petroleum spirits or dry cleaning fluid overnight to get the plasticky middle out.

3 Open up an earring clip to 90 degrees. Glue the bottle cap to the clasp half of the clip, with superglue.

4 Take a screw-together necklace fastener and remove the hook from the half of the fastener with a hole in it. Stick this half of the fastener to the flat half of the earring clip.

5 Stick a miniature candle in the hole in the necklace fastener.

A selection of miniature food: the cabbages and corn are made by putting brussel sprouts and the tips of baby sweetcorns in a microwave oven to dry them out and shrink them and the bread is made from real bread dough. The rest of the food is made from Fimo.

Making Orange Trees

1 Make miniature oranges from Fimo (see Making Food).

2 Take a piece of dried lichen (from model shops) and wind it loosely round a small twig. Secure it with rubber glue. Tease the lichen into shape and trim it with scissors if necessary.

3 Stick the oranges onto the tree with rubber glue. It might be easier to do this with tweezers.

4 Soften a lump of floral clay in your hands, and push it into a small plastic tub. Stick the tree into the floral clay. Cover the floral clay with pale browny green lichen.

Assembling the Room

The table is set for Thanksgiving dinner. Crockery, silverware and glasses are all from a doll house shop. The food, including the turkey and pumpkin soup, is on the table and on the sideboard.

RUSTIC BREAKFAST ROOM

The breakfast room, with its trompe-l'oeil walls and rustic twiggy furniture, almost suggests a room outside in the open air. The trompe-l'oeil, with its leaf-covered trellis and balustrades and its distant view of the landscape is based on this painting in the Royal Collection although I have simplified it. The effect is surprisingly easy to achieve and, because it is done on sheets of paper rather than directly onto the walls, any mistakes can easily be corrected. This design does, however, only really work in a square room.

Walls and Ceiling

1 Cut out a long strip of lightweight construction paper - it should be long enough to cover all the walls of the room. Cut out a second piece to fit the ceiling.

2 On a metal plate, make a puddle of white poster paint diluted with plenty of water. Place squeezes of ultramarine, burnt umber and cypress green watercolors on the edge of the plate. Mix a dab of ultramarine into the puddle to get a pale sky-blue wash.

3 Paint the wash roughly onto the cartridge paper for the walls with a large soft brush - the paper will get very wet and absorb the color. Darken the paint slightly and apply to the top of the paper, where the sky is darker. Blend the colors by dipping the brush in water and washing more water onto the paper.

4 Take a cotton rag and gently dab the paper to give it a more cloudy look and to break up some of the brush marks.

5 Repeat steps 3 and 4 on the ceiling, using a slightly darker blue wash than the walls. This should be darkened further for the center of the ceiling - but only slightly.

6 Add a little burnt umber to the wash to give it a gray tinge and paint some hazy, sketchy clouds onto the walls and ceiling. Again blend them in by brushing on more water, and dabbing the paper with a rag. None of this painting needs to be at all precise - it is just to give an impression of a nice day outside.

7 Add a touch more ultramarine and burnt umber to achieve a blue-gray wash, and sketch in some mountains - they should be quite small to create the impression of distance.

8 Mix in some cypress green to get a greeny gray and sketch in some trees and perhaps a bit of grass. Keep thinning down the wash so that it is really watery, and keep blending the colors and dabbing them with the rag to make them paler if necessary. Leave to dry for 1-2 hours. Trim the paper to fit the walls.

9 Cut lengths of cornice, dado and baseboard to fit each wall. Miter the ends (see page 11) and apply a coat of primer. When they are dry, apply a coat of pale gray emulsion to them all.

10 Cut out a piece of tracing paper to fit two walls of the room. Draw six equal arches across the tracing paper using a ruler for the pillars and a compass to draw the arched tops. The arches should almost reach the top of the paper, but leave room for the cornice above them. Then draw a balustrade below the height of the dado - and remember there will be a baseboard below it. If you don't want to draw the balustrade freehand, you could trace over a picture of one.

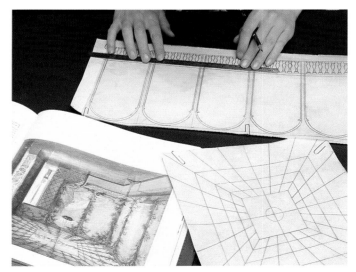

11 Transfer the tracing onto the wall paper for the first two walls. Then turn the tracing paper over, and transfer it again for the other two walls.

12 Cut a piece of tracing paper to fit the ceiling exactly. Divide it into quarters, and then eighths, by drawing in the diagonals. Draw four more squares inside each other, with the distances between them getting smaller, so that there is a central square approximately 2 inches square. Next, divide each eighth of the square paper into equal thirds, and draw in the lines from the edge of the paper to the innermost square. Finally, draw a small circle in the center. Transfer this tracing onto the ceiling paper.

13 Color the arches and balustrades with felt pens. You will need several gray pens - try to use browny shades of gray for a more realistic stone color. First, color in the arches, trellis and balustrades with a thick pale gray pen. Don't color the top or bottom of the balustrade as the baseboard and dado will be there.

14 Next, take a thinner-tipped pen - a slightly brownier gray - and outline the pillars and balustrades, and draw in an extra line in the middle of each pillar and a curved line on the bulge of the balustrade to make them look more rounded.

15 Then draw in the shadows of the pillars, arches, balustrades and trellis using a thin-tipped darker browny gray pen. Decide where the imaginary sun is and draw in the shadows away from the sun. If you have never done this before, it is a good idea to work out the positions of the shadows on a rough piece of paper, because it is important to get them in the right place and they must be consistent all around the room.

16 Mix a pale leafy green paint, consisting of white poster paint tinted with raw umber and olive green watercolors.

17 Place the cornice, dado rail and baseboard onto the paper in their correct positions.

18 Take a piece of natural sponge and dab it very lightly in the paint, so that there is not much paint on the sponge. Then dab the sponge onto the paper, turning it around the pillars and balustrades to give the impression of leaves growing up them. Also, dab the sponge over the baseboard and cornice and then around the trellis on the ceiling - so that the leaves are climbing all over the room.

19 Darken the paint slightly with some indigo watercolor to get a more bluey green, and repeat the process so that the color of the leaves varies. Be very careful not to have too much paint on the sponge and always dab the sponge very lightly on the paper. Leave to dry.

Making 'Twiggy' Furniture

1 To make the chairs you will need a selection of twigs ⅛ inch thick. Try to find some straight twigs and some which are more knobbly - oak twigs are best. For each chair you need two 1-inch lengths of knobbly twig for the front legs, two 2-inch lengths of knobbly twig for the back legs and back of the chair, eight 1-inch lengths of straight twig for the supports between the legs, one 1-inch length of knobbly twig for the top of the back and one knobbly twig to make a diagonal across the back of the chair.

2 Stick all the parts of the chair together with wood glue.

3 The seat is made from needlepoint canvas. Dye the fabric with a dirty brown watercolor and leave to dry. Cut out a square of the fabric slightly larger than the seat and cut little squares in each corner so that it fits round the legs. Stretch the fabric over the seat, fold the edges onto the bottom and secure with PVA.

4 Tables are made in a similar way - the tabletops are thin slices of a medium-sized branch - flower and dried flower shops sell these. Cut some twigs for legs, and stick them to the top.

Assembling the Room

Stick the wallpaper and ceiling paper into the room with PVA. Lay wooden planks, stained dark brown, across the floor. Then, stick the cornice, baseboard and dado rail onto the walls, also with PVA. Place the furniture into the room. The table has been set for breakfast on Easter Day, with wooden cups and saucers and bowls made from acorn cups. The eggs are made from Fimo (see Making Food, page 60). Bowls of crocuses and chickens (from a toy shop, and painted white) sitting in little baskets are placed on the side tables.

ITALIAN VILLA FAÇADE

This rather standard doll house, with its curved pediment can be transformed into an Italian country villa. The walls are roughly painted with a pinky terracotta wash, and the terracotta-tiled roof is made by sticking strips of painted corrugated cardboard onto the roof. Try to find a picture of a real terracotta-tiled roof as reference for the colors.

Washing the Walls

1 Apply a coat of white primer to all surfaces except the roof, but including the chimneys.

2 Mix a paint consisting of white emulsion or distemper tinted with crimson, burnt sienna and raw sienna gouache colors to achieve an orange-pink terracotta color. Thin the paint down with quite a lot of water so that it is more of a wash than a paint.

3 Paint the terracotta-colored wash onto the walls quite roughly with a small house paintbrush or a hog's hair brush. Use big sweeping brushstrokes, and vary the direction of the strokes to give it an authentic 'washed' look. Leave the windows, door, door frame and moldings white. Leave to dry.

4 Mix a dark green paint, consisting of green semigloss tinted with viridian, lemon chrome and black. Paint the door with this.

Terracotta Roof

1 Mix a darker terracotta paint than you used for the walls by tinting white primer with raw sienna and burnt sienna. Apply this paint to the corrugated side of a large piece of corrugated cardboard. Make sure that the paint gets right into all the ridges. Paint the chimney stacks with this terracotta paint.

2 Cut the cardboard into strips about 1¹/4 inches wide. Cut one strip about 2¹/2 inches wide to fold over the top of the roof onto both the front and back. Trim the strips so they fit the roof.

3 Apply a layer of PVA to the bottom of one side of the roof, and stick the first strip onto the roof. Apply more PVA above the strip and along the top of the strip and stick the next strip down so that it overlaps the first one by about ¹/4 inch.

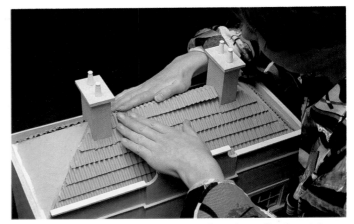

4 Continue sticking the strips of cardboard on all sides of the roof - try to keep them lined up all the way round, and trim the strips to fit around the chimney stacks. Finally, stick down the wide strip which folds over the top of the roof.

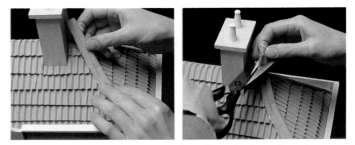

5 Cut four lengths of corrugated cardboard, along the ridges, which are two ridges wide. Trim them so they are the right length to run down the four corners on the roof. Stick them onto the corners, so they cover the edges of the strips of tiles.

6 Pour some of the terracotta paint used in step 1 onto a metal plate and place squeezes of Chinese orange, burnt sienna, crimson and black on the edge of the plate. Add dabs of these colors to darken the paint, and splodge it randomly on the tiles with a small house paintbrush. Alter the color regularly by adding more of one of the colors, and keep applying it randomly to the tiles, until the roof looks really weathered.

SCANDINAVIAN BEDROOM

A typically Scandinavian room tends to be very simple: sparsely decorated and furnished in cool soft grays, whites, blues or greens, with slightly faded fabrics and bare pine floorboards. This bedroom is typical of the style, with pale blue walls, small-checked green and white gingham fabrics and simple, but elegant furniture, hand-painted in subtly contrasting colors. A characteristic feature is the tall tiled stove for heating the room.

Walls and Ceiling

1 Apply a coat of white primer to the walls and ceiling. When they are dry, lightly sand them down.

2 On a plate, mix a pale blue-green paint, consisting of white distemper (if you can't get distemper use matt white emulsion), tinted with of indigo, raw umber and burnt umber gouache.

3 Starting on one of the side walls, apply the paint evenly to all the walls, brushing it out in all directions. Leave to dry. If the white undercoat is still showing through, apply a second coat.

4 Apply a coat of white emulsion to the ceiling.

5 Choose a very simple cornice without much decoration for this room. Cut it into lengths that fit the walls and miter the ends using a miniature miter box and saw (see page 11).

6 Apply a coat of white primer to the cornice, door and window. When they are dry, sand down lightly and apply a coat of white emulsion. Leave to dry.

7 Stick the cornices into the room with PVA or double-sided tape. Put the door and window into their frames.

8 Cut lengths of simple baseboard to fit the walls and miter the ends. Prime them and sand down lightly when they are dry.

9 Mix a dirty creamy-yellow paint, consisting of white emulsion tinted with raw umber, indigo and lemon chrome. Apply this paint to the baseboards. Leave to dry.

Floorboards

These are made by painting and graining a strip of balsawood, and then cutting it into miniature planks. You will need a strip 3/32 inch thick, about 3 inches wide and 18 inches long.

1 On a plate, mix matt white paint with dabs of black, burnt umber, raw umber and lemon chrome oil paints to achieve a pale woody color. Thin this down with petroleum spirit - it should be fairly watery. Apply this to the wood, so that it soaks in and allows the grain to show through.

2 Darken the paint with a little more black, burnt umber and raw umber. Dip a 3/4-inch fan brush into the paint, and then wipe it on a rag to separate the bristles.

3 Draw the brush over the wood, twisting it as you do so, thus using both the side and face of the brush, and then loop it back in the opposite direction to create the impression of graining and knots. The grain should be simple since the floor is supposed to be old pine. When you have to lift the brush off the wood twist it round and lift it off sideways, leaving as fine a line as possible.

4 When the whole sheet has been grained add another layer of darker graining to give it more texture. Darken the paint with more black, burnt umber and raw umber, and apply with the fan brush. You want quite a lot of graining so that, when the wood is cut into planks, each one looks really woody. If you are worried about over-doing the graining at this stage, wait and see what it looks like when the planks are cut up, and add more grain then.

5 Using the last darkest mixture of paint, paint in the knots in the loops that you have made in the graining. Leave to dry.

6 The floorboards will be laid from the back to the front of the room, so measure the depth of the room. Using a craft knife and a metal ruler, cut the wood into strips 3/4 inch wide and long enough to fit the depth of the room. When you have all the planks cut some into two pieces. These can be joined together on the floor to look more realistic.

7 The planks can either by nailed to the floor using very small nails, or stuck down with PVA. If you use PVA, paint in little gray nailheads afterwards for a more authentic look. When you are sticking them down, you may find that the last plank doesn't fit exactly - if so, mark it at either end, and trim off any extra using a metal ruler and a craft knife. You will also need to cut a space in one of the side planks to make room for the door frame.

8 Stick the baseboards onto the walls with PVA adhesive or double-sided tape.

Furniture

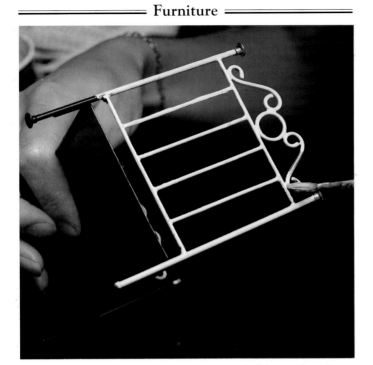

1 The furniture for the bedroom is from a doll house shop. It is very simple, and I have repainted it to suit the style of the room. Mix a creamy off-white paint, consisting of white semigloss tinted with raw umber, black and lemon chrome - make enough for two coats. Paint all the furniture with an even coat, using a small paintbrush, and leave to dry. Apply a second coat.

2 The fabric for the drapes and chair covers is a checked green-and-white gingham. For a slightly faded look dip the fabric in a mixture of matt white paint and turpentine and let it dry.

3 To make the chair covers, cut out two pieces of gingham which are the same shape but slightly larger than the chair back. Cut little holes at the corners for the legs. Sew the two pieces of fabric together on three sides, and hem the bottom and the leg holes. Turn the cover the right way out, thread ties through the hems around the leg holes, and put it over the chair back.

4 Make another cover for the cushion, with ties at each corner to go around the legs, and fit it over the chair cushion.

5 The stool cushion can be covered in a similar way and put back into the stool. To finish it off, stick a piece of cord or braid around the cushion.

Making a Stove

1 The stove is made from the cardboard tube of a paper towel roll. When the stove stands in the room it should almost reach the ceiling, so if the tube is too tall, cut it down to size.

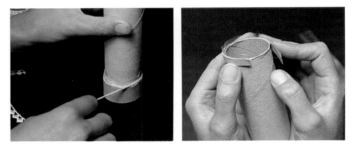

2 First make the base of the stove. Cut two pieces of medium-weight cardboard 1 inch wide and long enough to encircle the tube so that the ends meet but do not overlap. Wind the first piece around one end of the tube and stick it down with glue or double-sided tape. Stick the second piece of cardboard on top of the first, making sure that this join does not line up with the first one. Stick a piece of cord round the tube directly above the base to create a convex molding. Then, cut another piece of card 1/4 inch wide and wind it round the other end of the tube. Stick it down with glue or double-sided tape.

3 The top of the stove is made from the lid of a small tin. Stick the tin lid on top of the tube with lots of glue.

4 To make the moldings at the top of the stove, find two lengths of thick lace or eyelet fabric with different patterns which are long enough to encircle the tube without overlapping.

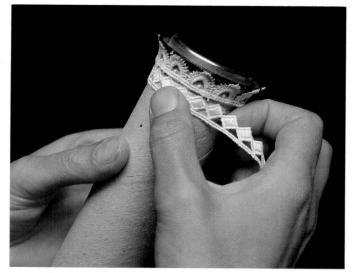

5 Stick the first piece onto the top of the tube, making sure that the top edge of the eyelet fabric curls up onto the side of the lid. Stick the second piece directly below it.

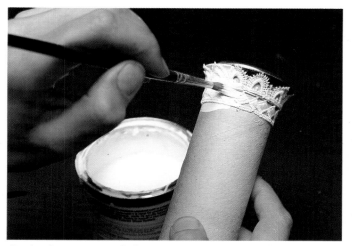

6 Apply two coats of white primer to the top and bottom of the stove to cover the moldings and the tin lid. Paint it on very thickly so that all the holes in the lace are filled.

7 After the second coat of primer has dried, apply two thick coats of varnish to give a shiny, slightly yellow look.

8 Cut a sheet of delft-tiled wallpaper (from doll's house shops) so that it fits round the stove between the two sets of moldings.

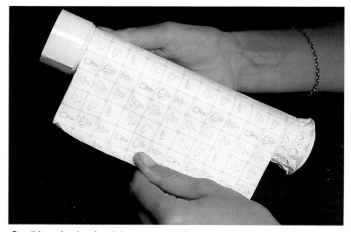

9 Glue the back of the paper with paper glue and wind it round the tube tightly, smoothing out any bubbles as you go.

10 Pencil the outline of the stove door, just above the bottom molding. It should be about 1 inch high and ³/4 inch wide.

11 Cut around the top, bottom and one side of the door, and score the remaining side so that the door can open and close.

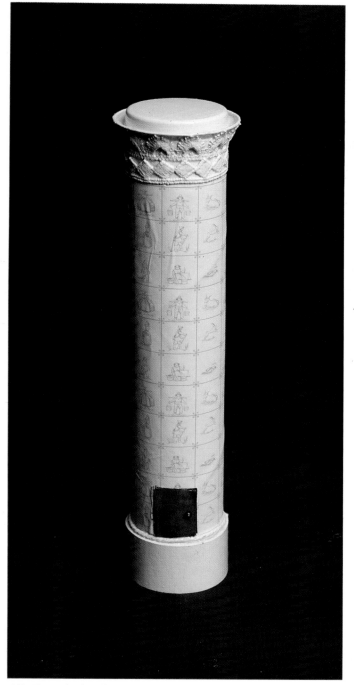

12 Paint both sides of the door with matt black paint. Make a door knob from a bronze bead and stick it on.

Assembling the Room

Make a simple pair of drapes, using the same material as you used for the chair and stool covers, and lengths of dowel painted white as curtain rails. (See Scottish Baronial Hall page 24 for method). Cover the mattress in finely striped cotton, and 'make the bed' by using scraps of white cotton to make sheets, blankets or duvets. Hang a mirror on one wall (see page 112 for gilding a mirror frame) and maybe a picture on another wall. The room does not want to be cluttered, so keep the furniture and decoration to the bare minimum.

SHAKER BEDROOM

The design of this rather old-fashioned American bedroom incorporates several typical Shaker features, such as the wooden chairs, which hang from pegs on the wall, and the pantry boxes piled up in the corner of the room. This is a simple but comfortable bedroom, without any unnecessary ornament. It is lit by a single lamp beside the bed.

Walls and Ceiling

1 Prepare the walls and ceiling by applying a coat of primer and, when they are dry, sanding them down lightly.

2 Tint white emulsion with a little raw umber gouache to get a creamy-white paint. Apply to the walls and ceiling. Leave to dry.

3 Cut lengths of baseboard to fit the walls and miter the ends. Apply a coat of primer to the baseboard and leave to dry.

4 Mix a chocolate-brown paint, consisting of black semigloss and bright scarlet semigloss. Apply to the baseboard. This paint is used for all the woodwork in the room so don't throw it away.

5 Prime the door and door frame. Leave to dry. Paint them with the chocolate-brown used above.

6 Next, make the rail and hooks on which the furniture will be hung. To do this, take a piece of hardwood 1/8 inch thick. Cut a strip 1/4 inch wide with a craft knife. Measure the length of the walls and cut the strip of wood into appropriate lengths. This rail will hang at the height of the top of the door frame, so you don't need to allow any wood for the door frame area.

7 Make pencil marks in the middle of the strip 1 inch apart. Then, using a bradawl make a hole on each of these marks.

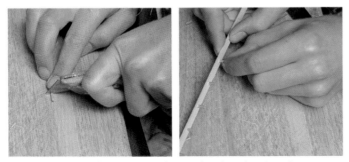

8 Make the hooks from wooden cocktail sticks. Cut the pointed ends of the cocktail sticks with a pair of scissors and throw them away. Cut the cocktail stick into 1/4-inch lengths. Push the little pegs into the holes to make sure that they fit. You might have to enlarge the hole a little bit more with the bradawl. When they fit, dip one end of the peg into some wood glue and then push it into the hole. Wipe away any excess glue.

9 Apply primer to the rail and pegs. Leave to dry. Paint them with the dark brown that you used for the door. Leave to dry.

10 Stick the rails onto the walls, at the height of the top of the door frame, with PVA adhesive.

Floor

1 Take a length of 1/8-inch-thick hardwood, and cut it into strips that are approximately 1 inch wide - they need not be exactly the same width. The planks will be laid across the room, so measure the width of the room, and cut the planks to fit.

2 Stain the planks with wood stainer. When they are dry, stick the floorboards into the room with wood glue. Finally, stick the baseboard onto the walls with PVA.

Furniture

The chairs, which hang on pegs on the wall, were bought in a doll house shop. They are very simple, and are painted with oil colors and varnish to look old and slightly battered.

1 Pour some varnish onto a metal plate, and put little squeezes of the appropriate-colored oil paints around the rim. Since I intended to paint the chairs a woody-brown, I used squeezes of raw umber and black; but if you decide to have colored chairs instead, you will obviously mix different colors with the varnish. Add little dabs of your oil paints to the varnish. When you are happy with the color test it on the chair and see how it looks. Wipe it off with a rag and white spirit if you don't like it.

2 Paint the colored varnish onto the chairs with a small (and preferably old) paintbrush. Leave to dry.

Patchwork Quilt

To make the quilt by sewing together lots of tiny little squares is both boring and time consuming. A quicker and easier way to make a doll house quilt is to take three pieces of different fabric, cutting them into strips and weaving the strips into a patchwork.

1 Try to find three pieces that have very different patterns and colors to give the quilt as much variety as possible. Use quite thick cotton or polished cotton - if it is too thin it will fray easily. Fabric samples from decorators' shops are ideal.

2 Cut one piece into strips ³/₁₆ inch wide - cut along the weave to stop it fraying. Stick one end of each strip to a piece of masking tape, keeping the strips right next to each other.

3 Cut the other two pieces of fabric into ³/₁₆-inch strips and weave them through the first strips in alternate rows. Push the strips right up against each other so that there are no gaps.

4 Continue doing this until the quilt is the right size for the bed. Press the quilt onto a piece of iron-on interfacing that is the same size, to keep all the weaving in position.

5 Cut out a piece of fabric exactly the same size as the quilt - this will form the back of the quilt. Sew three sides of the quilt and its backing together to make a bag - they must be sewn front-to-front so you can turn it the right way out later. If possible, use a sewing machine for this job.

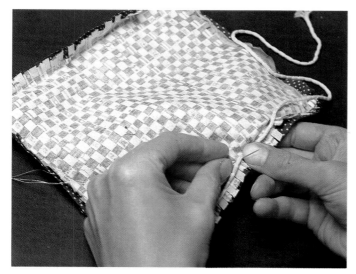

6 The sewn sides of the quilt need to be weighted so that they hang down over the sides of the bed. Take a length of curtain weight, and sew it outside the three machined seams.

7 Turn your 'bag' the right way out again, and sew up the last side by hand. This unweighted side will go at the pillow end of the bed. Finally press the quilt with a medium-hot iron.

It is often quite difficult to get fabrics to hang well in doll houses because they are not heavy enough, so curtain weights are very useful. They are for real curtains, and can be bought in two thicknesses from fabric shops and notions or haberdashery departments. For doll house fabrics, the thinner one is adequate. Another way of making fabrics hang properly is to starch them, although this does not look as natural.

Rag Rugs

1 You need several strands of cotton embroidery thread. If possible, use thread that is multicolored. Take three different-colored strands, knotted together at one end, and plait them. As you get towards the end of a thread, plait in another one. Continue until your plait is about a yard long - obviously the length of plait depends on the size of rug you want to make.

2 Use a piece of thick canvas or needlepoint canvas as the base for your rug. Spread some fabric glue or Copydex onto the base. Place one end of the plait in the middle of the glue, and slowly wind the plait around itself - either in a circle or in a rectangle.

3 Keep winding the plait around itself, adding more glue to the canvas when necessary, until it is the required size. Leave the end of the plait loose and carefully cut the canvas around the rug with a pair of scissors.

4 To trim the edges neatly, and to prevent the backing sticking out, wind the plait around one more time. You might need more glue for this. Fold the loose end of the plait under the rug and trim it. Secure the loose end onto the backing with glue.

Pantry or 'Shaker' Boxes

These circular or oval boxes are a very typical Shaker feature - make about half-a-dozen different-sized boxes to pile up in the bedroom.

1 To make the tops and bottoms of the Shaker boxes you need a piece of balsawood approximately ¹/₃₂ inch thick - or even thinner if you can get it. Use a bottle cap or a coin to draw circles onto the balsawood. Make sure that the circles for the top of the boxes are slightly larger than those for the bottom - about ¹/₈ inch bigger in diameter.

2 Cut round the circles with a craft knife - do this quite slowly and carefully to avoid splitting the wood. Any rough edges can be sanded down afterwards.

3 Then, take a piece of thin, floppy cardboard and cut it into strips. These will be bent round to form the sides of the boxes. The width of each strip (which will be the height of the side of the box) should be about the same as the diameter of the base to which it will be attached. The length of the strip must equal the circumference of the base, so wind it round the base and cut it.

4 Cut narrower strips of cardboard for the edges of the box lids. These should be about a quarter of the height of the side of the box. Cut the length to equal the circumference of the top.

5 Spread some PVA all around the outside edge of the circular base. Place the edge of the base on the wider strip of cardboard, and wind the cardboard tightly around to stick it to the base. Secure it temporarily with a piece of masking tape while the glue dries. Repeat this process with the lid of the box and its side. Remove the masking tape when the glue has dried.

6 When the glue has dried, paint the boxes with watercolors. They can be painted any color you like, but to look authentic they should be quite dirty, washed-out colors - bluey greens, grays and browns. All the colors have a little black or some kind of brown in them - either raw or burnt umber - to distress them. For example, the reddish one is a mixture of cadmium red and burnt umber; the yellowish one is raw sienna with a dash of black; the pinkish one is crimson, black and burnt umber; the green one is olive-green with a little raw umber and so on.

Assembling the Room

The room should feel quite homely without being too cluttered. Hang chairs, and maybe some miniature clothes on the pegs. The bed is a simple wooden bed, with its patchwork quilt. Miniature cushions, covered in a variety of fabrics, can be made for the bed. The fabrics tend to have quite strong colors and patterns - spots, stripes and checks. The furniture is all simple and wooden. The rag rugs are on the floor and the Shaker boxes piled up in a corner.

AN ENGLISH COUNTRY-HOUSE BEDROOM

This bedroom is decorated and furnished in a traditionally English style. It is almost formal, with its upholstered walls and canopy bed. The same small-patterned floral fabric is used to make the drapes and upholster the furniture and the painted wooden furniture picks out colors in the fabric. The details, such as the Staffordshire dogs on the mantelpiece and the porcelain jars on the carved brackets, are in keeping with the rather grand style of this bedroom.

Walls, Ceiling and Floor

1 Apply white primer to the walls and the ceiling. Leave to dry.

2 Mix a slightly off-white paint by tinting white emulsion with raw umber and raw sienna. Apply to the ceiling. Leave to dry.

3 Paint the inside of the fireplace black.

The fabric used to upholster the walls should have quite a small pattern - it probably shouldn't be bigger than 3/4-1 inch. Floral fabrics are very good for this sort of traditional English look. Lightweight upholstery fabric is best although you could use a medium-weight dressmaking fabric. In real rooms, when walls are upholstered the fabric is nailed to battens on each edge of the wall, and the nails are concealed by braid which is stuck around the edges of the room. In a doll house room it is easier to use double-sided tape as battens and then stick braid around the edges of the room.

4 Dye the braid to match a mid or dark color from the fabric using oil paints mixed with petroleum spirits. You will need enough to trim the walls, as well as the drapes and bed hangings. Dye it all at once as it is very difficult to achieve exactly the same color again. Leave to dry overnight.

5 Stick double-sided tape along every horizontal and vertical edge in the room, on both sides of corners, and around the fireplace, door and window.

6 Cut the fabric so that it is about 1/8 inch shorter than the height of the room and long enough to cover all the walls - you might need to sew two pieces of fabric together to get a piece long enough. If so, make sure that the pattern joins up at the seam, and press the seam open so that it lies flat. Also, try to position the seam so that it will fall in a corner of the room or on one side of the window, where it will not show too much.

7 Starting on a side wall place the fabric into the room, and slowly stick it onto the tape, keeping the fabric quite tightly stretched across the walls. Stick it right up to the ceiling at the top, so that it does not quite reach the floor. Make sure that it is stuck right into all the corners.

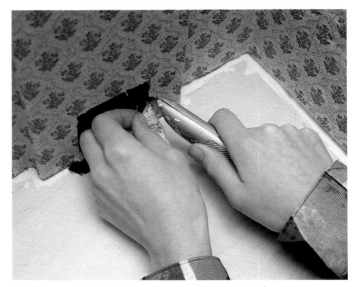

8 Cut out the fabric over the fireplace and window. Use a craft knife, and slowly cut round the shapes of the window and fireplace. Trim any loose threads with scissors.

9 Cut lengths of cornice and baseboard to fit the walls and miter the ends with a miniature miter box (see page 11). It is better to do this after the walls have been upholstered because the thickness of the fabric affects the lengths of the walls.

10 Apply a coat of white primer to the baseboard and cornice. Leave to dry. Prime the fireplace at the same time.

11 Tint some semigloss varnish with a little raw umber and raw sienna and apply to the fireplace, the cornice and the molding on top of the baseboard. This will give them a creamy colored glaze. Leave them all to dry.

12 Mix an off-black paint consisting of black, white and brown, and apply to the board of the baseboard. Leave to dry.

13 Stick the cornice and fireplace into the room with PVA adhesive. The baseboard will be stuck in after the carpet.

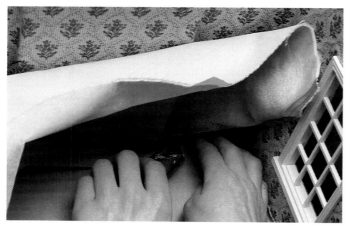

14 The carpet is made from creamy beige velvet (cotton or silk velvet are best). Place the fabric in the room and cut it to fit, taking care to trim around the chimney-breast and door frame.

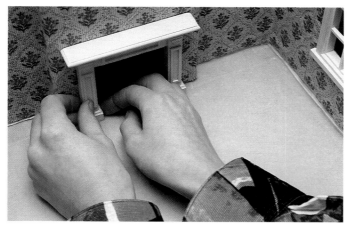

15 If the carpet has been cut accurately, it will not need glueing, but you could secure it with a little PVA or double-sided tape in the corners and the front edge of the room.

16 Stick the baseboard into the room with a little PVA taking care to apply the glue thinly to the middle of the baseboard so that it doesn't dribble down onto the carpet.

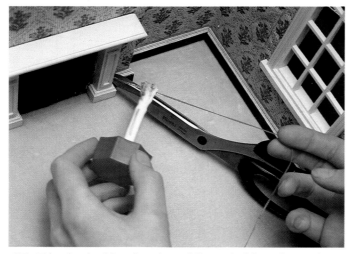

17 Take the dyed braid, and carefully apply fabric glue to the back. The braid should be very thin, ideally 1/12 inch, since braid in a real room is usually 1 inch wide. Stick it into the room directly below the cornice. Work quickly but carefully, because the Copydex dries quite quickly. Place the next piece of braid directly above the baseboard and around the fireplace and door.

A Canopy Bed

Doll house shops sell canopy beds, but you might want to redecorate and upholster it, as I have, to suit the style of your bedroom. The first step in transforming your canopy bed is to make a tester, which will be painted, and a sturdy wooden frame to support the tester and the frills and drapes.

1 Cut four lengths of dado rail to fit around the four posts. Miter the ends and glue them together with wood glue to make the tester. Cut three more pieces of dado 1 inch long, and glue them, back to front and upside down, in the center of the front and two sides of the tester to make small panels or quoins for the painted decoration.

2 Cut four lengths of hardwood 1/8 thick and 3/4 inch wide to fit just inside the four posts of the bed. Miter the ends and stick them together with wood glue to make a rectangular supporting frame. You will need to cut off the corners of the frame so that it can sit inside the posts.

3 Apply a coat of primer to the tester. Leave to dry.

4 Paint the tester off-black using the same paint that was used for the baseboard (step 12 above) and leave to dry.

5 Pour a little petroleum spirit onto a plate and mix in some raw sienna and white oil paints to achieve quite a dark cream color - when you are painting onto black, the paint needs to be darker than you think. Using a very thin sable brush, paint a curvy stalk along each side of the tester, but not on the quoins.

6 Then, using the same cream paint, add little flowers on either side of the stalk - these do not need to be precise at all - they are really just small round blobs.

7 Add a little burnt umber to the paint to make it browner. Paint leaves onto the stalk - make the leaves radiate out from the quoins so everything points away from the center of each side of the tester. Also, use this browner paint to emphasize the center of the flowers by painting a little circle in each one to make them look more rounded.

8 Decorate the quoins by painting a naked lady or a pot or an urn on each one. If you don't feel confident painting these freehand, you can trace the shape from a book and transfer it to the quoin. The painting does not need to be too precise.

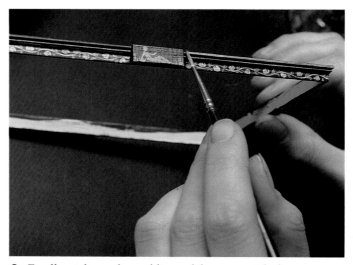

9 Finally, pick out the moldings of the tester with the creamy-colored paint - use the smallest sable brush you have for this.

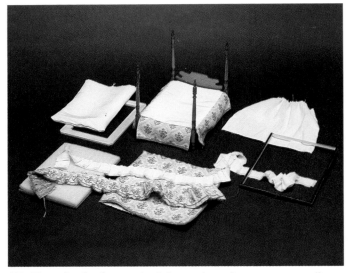

10 To make the fringe which hangs from the tester, you will need a long strip of the same fabric that you used for the walls - 1¹/₂ inches wide. If necessary sew the strips together so that it is long enough to go round three sides of the tester when it has been pleated. Sew a strip of the ribbon that you dyed earlier onto the fabric ¹/₄ inch from the bottom with a sewing machine. Pull out the threads underneath the ribbon to fray the fabric and thus create a fringe.

11 Gather the fabric every inch or so to make a small box-pleat. Secure the pleat with a pin, and then sew it in place ¹/₂ inch from the top of the fabric. When all the pleats have been sewn in, iron the fabric to flatten them, and remove the pins.

12 Make a simple valance by sewing pieces of the same fabric onto a a piece of cream lining which covers the bed. Trim the bottom of the valance with the ribbon which was dyed to match the fabric. If you are using thin fabric you could make a gathered valance, but if the fabric is too thick the pleats will become puffy and look untidy.

13 Make a simple back drape for the bed from the patterned fabric. It should be long enough to reach the floor, and about 2 inches wider than the bed so that it folds round onto the two sides. Trim the back drape with dyed ribbon. If the fabric is thin, you could make a gathered back drape. If you do this, you should also tie the drape to the bed posts with little tie backs.

14 Make a lining for the back drape from cream silk or cotton. Cut the fabric into a rectangle, which is as long as the height from the floor to the top of the posts and twice as wide as the bed. Gather the fabric at the top so that it is about 2 inches wider than the width of the bed.

15 Make a bag from cream silk or cotton to cover the supporting frame. Put the frame inside the bag - it should fit quite tightly inside - and sew up the open end.

16 Make a lining for the tester fringe from a piece of cream lining fabric which has been gathered into box pleats. Sew the fringe and the lining together using a sewing machine.

17 Stick the lining of the back drape onto the back of the support with fabric glue. About an inch of this lining will fold round and be stuck onto either side of the frame.

18 Next, stick the back drape on top of the lining with fabric glue - this will also fold round onto the sides of the frame.

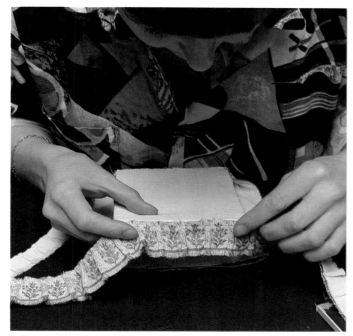

19 Then, stick the frill onto the supporting frame. Apply fabric glue all around the edge of the frame. Start sticking the fringe in the middle of the front, making sure that a box pleat is right in the center. Working out from the middle, stick the fringe all the way round the frame, on top of the bits of the drape that are folded round from the back, and secure it at the back of the supporting frame with a good squeeze of fabric glue. Trim off any extra fabric at the back.

22 The mattress is a piece of foam, cut to fit the bed. Cover the mattress with thinly striped fabric, and sew through the mattress in several places to give the impression of mattress buttons.

20 Apply some PVA to the inside of the tester. Place the frame inside the top of the posts. Then ease the painted tester over the frame, on the outside of the posts, so that it sandwiches the posts and layers of fabric between it and the supporting frame.

21 Rearrange the lining of the back drape so that it hangs down in front of the bedhead.

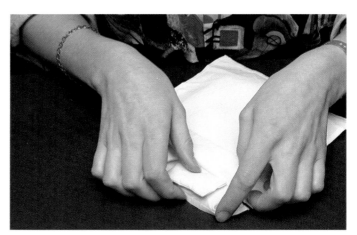

23 Make the bed with sheets, pillows and blankets and cover it with a cream-colored bedspread.

Assembling the Room

The bedroom is furnished in a very traditional way. The drapes are made from the same fabric as the walls. An armchair, in the corner of the room, and the stool in front of the dressing table are also upholstered with the same fabric. Bedside tables are made by making a small wooden box, and sticking cocktail sticks onto the four corners to support a square shelf. The tables are then primed and painted cream, with pale green inset panels. The dressing-table is similarly painted, and is placed in front of the window. Miniature books are placed on the bedside tables, and china pots and dogs (made from air-dry modeling clay) sit on the mantelpiece. The paintings on the wall are made by fitting a gilded frame around part of a museum postcard. Finishing touches include a breakfast tray (the cups and saucers are also made from air-dry modeling clay) and a newspaper on the bed.

ETRUSCAN BATHROOM

The style of this bathroom is based on an eighteenth-century interpretation of the Etruscan style but, with its clear, clean colors and geometric shapes, the effect is almost modern. The trademarks of the Etruscan style are in the use of color - duck-egg blue predominating, combined with burnt orange, buff and soft black. The mosaic floor adds to the cool atmosphere, and provides an extra texture in a room which is otherwise almost spartan in its lack of furniture. If you wish to light this room, you could wire in a bulb behind the bathtub alcove - or have your bath in the dark.

Floor

1 Cut out a piece of construction paper to fit the floor exactly.

2 Find a suitable design for a mosaic or patterned floor from a book or a magazine. If it is not the right size for the room, it can be reduced or enlarged on a photocopier.

3 Trace the pattern and transfer it onto the construction paper. (You could short-cut these three steps by cutting your photocopy to fit the floor and using that as the base.)

5 Sprinkle grains of rice all around the edges of the pattern. Thin some PVA with water, to the consistency of single cream. Apply two coats with a small soft brush, pushing it between the lentils so that it soaks underneath them, holds them in position and varnishes them. Stick the floor into the room with PVA.

4 The mosaic is created by arranging lentils on the patterned paper. It is best to have three bags of lentils, each a different color: orange, black and white for example. Use the flattest you can find. Before sticking them down, work out which colors go where. Spray a generous layer of Spray Mount onto the paper. Starting in the centre of the pattern and working out, arrange the lentils on the paper. It is probably easier to use tweezers rather than fingers for this. Continue adding lentils until the pattern is complete. If the adhesive loses its stick, spray on more or warm the paper to reactivate the glue.

Walls and Arch

1 Cut out a simple hardwood arch to fit exactly into the room.

2 Apply a coat of white primer to the arch, the walls and the ceiling. When they are dry, sand them down lightly.

3 Mix a pale blue-gray paint, consisting of matt white emulsion tinted with small quantities of indigo and raw umber. Apply this paint to all the walls and one side of the arch. Make sure that you paint the rim of the arch as well. Leave to dry.

4 Stick the arch into the room with wood glue. Position it about 2 inches from the back wall - the bath will be behind the arch, so make sure you leave enough room for it.

5 Cut lengths of cornice to fit all the walls, and baseboards and dados for the two side walls. Miter the ends of the cornice, and spray a coat of primer onto all these moldings. Leave to dry.

6 Cut strips of orange construction paper to fit between the baseboard and dado on the side walls. Stick them in with PVA.

7 Paint the baseboard black, the cornice, door and door frame off-white and the dado buff-color. Leave to dry. Stick them in with PVA - the dado is at the height of the top of the bathtub.

Panels for the Walls

Rather than painting panels directly onto the walls, I made them by cutting out pieces of colored paper, assembling them on my work-table and then sticking them into the room. It is much easier, and any mistakes can easily be corrected.

1 You need several pieces of different-colored thin construction paper - duck-egg blue, orange, buff and black. These can either be bought, or made by painting white construction paper with watercolors. You will also need black and orange felt-tip pens, and a draftsman's template with circles, ovals and hexagons.

2 Measure the walls where the panels will be stuck - one on either side of the arch, one on either side of the basin and one on either side of the fireplace. The panels should be set in 1/4 inch all round from the edges of the walls, and the same distance above the dado rail. Mark out the sizes of the panels on the blue paper, and cut them out.

3 Using a ruler and an orange felt-tip pen, draw a line around the edge of each blue panel. Then, draw a second set of orange lines about 1/8 inch inside the first line.

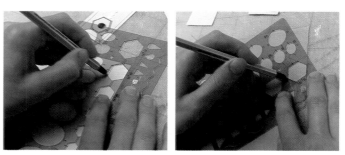

4 Next, draw the circles, hexagons and ovals which decorate the panels, using the draftsman's template. For the top and bottom of each panel you need a large orange hexagon, a smaller buff hexagon with a black outline to fit inside that, and a small black circle in the center. For the middle of each panel you need a large buff oval with an orange outline, a slightly smaller black oval and a blue oval which is smaller still. The sizes of these shapes will vary according to the widths of the blue panels.

5 If the shapes have a different-colored outline, mark the shape from the template with the appropriate-colored felt-tip pen and cut around these lines.

6 Cut out all the ovals, circles and hexagons.

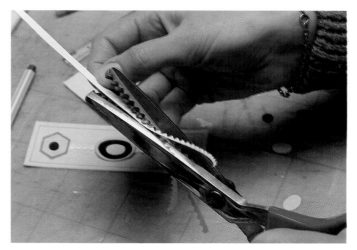

7 Next, make a thin zig-zag 'ribbon' to run down the center of each panel and join the medallions. Cut a thin strip of white paper and fold it in half. Using a pair of pinking scissors, cut the folded strip of paper so that the zig-zags do not quite reach the fold. Open the strip of paper out and press it flat.

8 Trim the zig-zag ribbon so that its length is about 3/4 inch shorter than the length of the panel.

9 Glue the zig-zag down the center of the panel. The ends of the zig-zag should be about 1/4 inch inside the inner orange line.

10 Stick the colored shapes onto the zig-zag ribbon in the order described in step 4 using paper glue. The top and bottom medallions should cover the ends of the ribbon, and be about 1/8 inch inside the inner orange line. The middle medallion is positioned halfway between the other two.

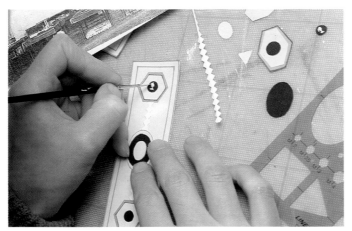

11 Paint decorations - a head or an urn, perhaps - on the black circles for the top and bottom medallions, and a slightly larger decoration - maybe an ancient Roman in a toga - in the blue oval for the middle medallion. Use white poster paint and a thin sable brush. Copy from a book, and practise on a piece of paper first. If you are not confident about painting freehand, lightly trace on a design and then paint over that. The decorations do not need to be too precise - just a vague silhouette of the shape.

12 Lightly mark the walls with a pencil to indicate the positions of each of the panels.

13 Stick the panels onto the walls with PVA adhesive. If the constrction paper is very thin, stick them with rubber glue. Make sure that the panel is absolutely straight before sticking it down.

Making Banquettes

1 The two banquettes for the back corners of the bathroom are each made from two pieces of balsawood. Their height should be the same as that of the bathtub. The seat of the banquette is a piece of balsawood 1/4 inch thick cut into a right-angled triangle, with the two equal sides being about 1/2 inch longer than the width of the arch base. Cut off the two acute angles of the triangle at 45 degrees to the edges that will be against the wall, so that the top of the banquette fits exactly into the corner.

2 The base of the banquette is a block of balsawood 1/3 inch thick. Its height should be the height of the bathtub minus 1/4 inch (to allow for the top of the banquette) and it should be the same width as the length of the diagonal edge of the top.

3 Stick the two pieces of balsawood together with PVA.

4 Cover the banquettes with cream silk. You can use other fabrics, but try to avoid synthetics as they don't hang well. Cut a 5-inch square of fabric, and fold it in half diagonally so that it is triangular. Press the fabric, so the fold is sharp.

5 Using a sewing machine, sew two lines of orange stitching along the diagonal edge.

6 Place the triangle of fabric over the banquette, so that the diagonal, orange-hemmed edge will touch the floor.

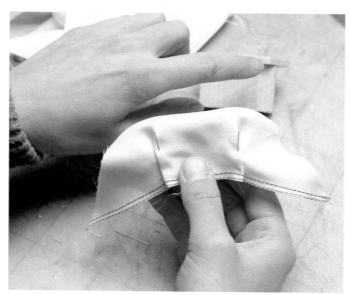

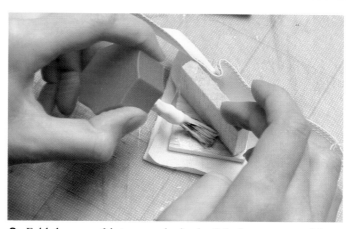

8 Fold the extra fabric onto the back of the banquette and fix it with fabric glue. Then, carefully hold the banquette over the spout of a boiling kettle. The steam will dampen the fabric, and when it dries will set the pleats. Remove the pins when it is dry.

7 Fold and pin two outward-facing pleats on the front corners.

9 Trim the banquette with orange cord.

Assembling the Room

Place the banquettes in the back corners in front of the arch - they are the same height as the bathtub and the dado. The bathtub and basin, which can be bought from doll house shops, are put in position; the bathtub behind the arch. The mirror above the basin is made from a circular mirror from a make-up compact. Stick a piece of eyelet fabric around the edge of the mirror to form the molding of the frame. Apply a thick coat of primer to the eyelet fabric. Leave to dry. Apply a coat of brick-colored paint on top. Leave to dry. Finally paint the frame with gold paint and rub the paint off some of the projecting moldings to distress the frame. Leave to dry. Attach the mirror to the wall with a double-sided adhesive pad. The finishing touch is miniature towels, made from white velvet, folded up on the banquettes.

A VICTORIAN SHOP FRONT

I have decided to decorate the façade of this Victorian shop in brick and stucco, with the bottom of the first-floor windows as the dividing line between them, and a slate roof. This is in keeping with real shops of this period. The sheets of brick and slate are from doll house shops, but they have been 'weathered' to look more realistic. The lines between the stucco slabs are drawn with felt-pens.

Walls and Roof

1 Apply a coat of white primer to the outside of the house from the bottom of the first floor windows to the ground. Also, prime all the window frames, window ledges and the chimney stack, chimney pots and the gables. Leave to dry.

2 Mix a cream-colored paint, consisting of white emulsion tinted with raw umber watercolor or gouache. Apply a coat of this paint to the all the parts that you have primed, except the gables, chimney stack and chimney pots. Leave to dry.

3 Mix a brick-colored paint, consisting of white emulsion tinted with raw sienna, burnt sienna, raw umber and black. Apply to the chimney pots and then paint their insides black.

4 Take the sheets of brick, and hold them against the top parts (which have not been primed) of the front and sides of the shop. Mark the edges of the building and cut the bricks to fit the walls.

5 Hold the brick sheets against the shop again, and mark in the positions of each window. Cut around the window. Don't forget to cut around the window ledge as well.

6 Stick the brick sheets onto the front and sides of the shop with PVA adhesive.

7 Cut sheets of slate to fit the roof. Stick them on with PVA. Make sure that you cut carefully around the chimney stack. Mix a dark green paint consisting of black, raw umber, lemon chrome and viridian. Apply to the gables. Don't throw this paint away.

8   Stick bricks around the chimney stack with PVA adhesive.

9   On a plate, mix a foxy-colored varnish by tinting clear matt varnish with burnt sienna, raw sienna, black and white oil paints. Thin down with petroleum spirit to a milky consistency. Apply this roughly to the chimney pots and chimney stack.

10   Add a little lemon chrome to the varnish and more petroleum spirit if necessary - it should be quite watery. Apply the varnish roughly, with vigorous brush strokes, to one wall. Use a bristle brush to get right into the surface of the bricks. Vary the color from time to time by adding a little more of one of the colors - this will create the effect of weathering. Bunch up a piece of cotton rag and dab the wall, taking off some of the varnish as you go. Repeat on the other walls, one at a time.

11   On a metal plate, mix a browny-gray varnish by tinting clear matt varnish with dabs of burnt sienna, burnt umber, black and white. Thin with petroleum spirit to a milky consistency and apply it to the roof, using a bristle brush.

12   Vary the color from time to time by adding a little more of one of the colors to give the impression of weathering. Rag it straight away, as you did for the brick walls. Leave to dry.

13   To draw in the lines on the stucco you will need two permanent felt-tipped pens: a thick-tipped pale gray pen and fine-tipped darker gray pen. It is also a good idea to stick double-sided tape onto the back of your ruler so that it sticks to the wall as you are drawing the lines - this will stop the ruler slipping.

14   Mark the positions of the lines in pencil up the side of the building - you can always rub out any mistakes. The first horizontal line is at the height of the bottom of the window ledge. Above that the lines should be approximately $1^{1}/_{8}$ inches apart, but try to position them so that they line up with any moldings on the façade such as door or window frames.

15   Starting on the front of the building, draw in the horizontal lines with the thick pen. Leave a space for the keystones which fan out from the top of the window.

16   Draw in the thick lines for the keystones above the window, and join the horizontal line to the edge of the keystones. When the front is finished, draw in the thick lines on the side walls, making sure they join the lines on the front at the corners.

17 Using the fine-tipped darker gray pen and ruler, draw in thin lines - at the top of the thick pale gray lines and to the right of the thick lines of the keystones.

Naming the Shop

The best way of 'writing' the name above the shop is with Letraset.

1 Trace the Letraset letters onto tracing paper and hold the paper in position to check the size and spacing of the letters.

2 Draw a faint pencil line to show the position of the letters and mark its center.

3 Rub on the letters from the Letraset sheet. Start with the middle letter in the center of the pencil line and work outwards. Make sure that each letter is straight before rubbing it on. If you do make a mistake, lift off the Letraset with masking tape.

4 Rub on a Letraset number above the door.

5 Fix the letters with spray fixative to stop bits flaking off.

6 To make the name really stand out, highlight the shadows of the letters with oil-based gold paint. Use a very fine paintbrush and carefully paint in the shadows. Rest the edge of your hand on the house as you paint to keep it steady; go very slowly, so that you keep the lines sharp and even. Paint in the shadow of the number above the door. If you have not painted in shadows before, it is a good idea to work out where the gold lines must go on a piece of paper before you start painting.

7 Using the same green paint that you used for the gables (see step 7 above), pick out the moldings on the shop front. Apply it evenly with a sable brush to the door, the front ridges of the curved pediment, and the finials on top of the pediment.

EDWARDIAN HAT SHOP

This Edwardian hat shop has an air of understated sophistication and elegance. Its furnishings are very traditional: a glass-fronted cabinet and mahogany shelves, filled with scarves, rolls of fabric and ribbons; a chaise longue, upholstered in a subtly-striped fabric; a large mirror and, of course, plenty of hats arranged in the window and on hat stands.

Walls and Ceiling

1 Apply a coat of white primer to all the walls and the ceiling. When they are dry, sand them down lightly.

2 Mix a cream-colored paint, consisting of matt white emulsion tinted with raw umber and raw sienna. Apply to the walls.

3 Cut lengths of cornice, dado rail and baseboard to fit the walls. Miter the ends using a miniature miter box (see page 11). Make a door and door frame (see the Nursery, page 114).

4 Apply a coat of gray primer to all the moldings. At the same time, prime the door and door frame, and any pieces of furniture for the room - shelves, counter, chaise longue. Leave to dry.

5 Mix a deep brown glaze by tinting varnish with burnt umber, burnt sienna, black and white oils. Apply to the moldings and furniture, brushing out the paint in the one direction.

6 Darken the mixture by adding more black and, using a fan brush, apply it lightly over the glaze. This will create a series of thin veins - or grain - making them look like mahogany. Keep these veins quite straight when you paint them, but vary their widths by using the side of the brush as well. Leave to dry.

Floor

1 Make a template of the floor on a piece of newspaper.

2 Place the template on a piece of very pale gray felt, and cut out the felt. Apply a thin layer of all-purpose glue to the floor and stick the felt carpet in position.

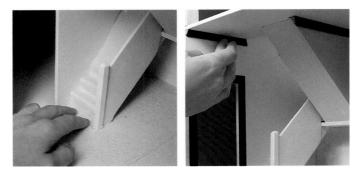

3 Cut out a strip of felt the same width as the staircase, and long enough to carpet the stairs. Apply a layer of glue to the stairs and stick the carpet down, taking care to push it right into the back of the treads. Then, stick the cornice, dado rail, baseboard, and door frame into the room with PVA. The dado should be approximately 2 inches above the floor. Put the door into the door frame.

The Window

The ledge inside the window is lined with white silk, and a shelf is made for displaying hats. The drapes are made from thin silk twisted around a pole and arranged so there is one swag in each window.

1 Take a length of very thin white silk (a thin silk scarf would do) and dip the scarf in cool tea. This will dye it a soft creamy color. Leave it to dry.

2 Twist both ends of the silk in opposite directions so that the silk becomes like a twisted rope. Carefully hold this twisted silk rope over the spout of a boiling kettle so that the steam dampens the silk, and soaks into all the creases. When it is quite damp, take the silk away and leave it to dry. When it dries the silk will keep its twisted shape and set the creases.

3 Cut a length of dowel long enough to fit the width of the windows. Apply a coat of white primer. Leave to dry.

4 Unwrap the silk and wind it round the pole three times to make three swags. The rest of the silk hangs down at either side.

5 Attach the curtain pole to the wall with small hooks hammered into the wall.

6 Tease and arrange the swags, so they hang well in the windows. Try not to let them get too puffy.

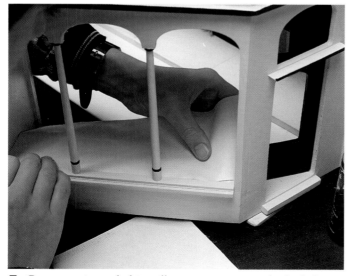

7 Cut out a piece of white silk or satin-cotton to fit the ledge inside the window. Iron fabric stiffener onto the back of the fabric to stop it fraying. Stick it onto the ledge with fabric glue.

8 The shelf to go in the window is made from balsawood ¹/₈ inch thick. Cut out one strip approximately 1 inch wide and 4 inches long, another strip the same length but ¹/₂ inch wide, and two strips 1 inch long and ¹/₂ inch wide. (The lengths of the long strips will vary according to the size of the window - but it should be about 1 inch shorter than the width of the window.)

9 Stick the pieces of wood together with wood glue so that you have what looks like half a box.

10 Cut out a piece of white fabric large enough to cover the shelf (use the same fabric as you used in step 7). Iron fabric stiffener onto the back to stop it fraying.

11 Apply fabric glue very thinly to the wood, and stick the fabric onto it - make neat tucks at the corners to fold the fabric round (like hospital corners when you are making a bed).

12 Place the covered shelf in the window.

Making Hats

You will need a wide variety of hats for the shop, but they are easy to make from fabric scraps. The best fabrics to use are felt or silk, and try to use as many different colors as possible.

1 To make the crown of almost any hat, simply dampen the fabric with boiling water, and stretch it over the end of a cork. Secure it with an elastic band and leave it to dry overnight.

2 To make a simple pill-box hat, remove the elastic band from the cork. Trim the excess fabric and wind another piece of fabric or ribbon, cut to the right width, around the hat - this could be a different color or it could be patterned. You might want to decorate the hat with a feather, or with a veil made from fine tulle. When the hat is finished, remove it from the cork.

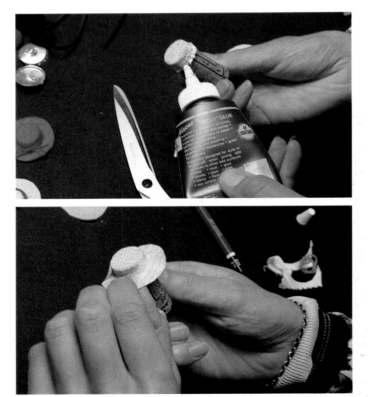

3 To make a brimmed hat, cut out a circle of fabric about 1 1/2 inches in diameter. Trim the circle into a slightly oval or head shape. If you are using silk, iron fabric stiffener onto the back. Cut a second circle inside the oval with a diameter slightly smaller than that of the cork. Remove the elastic band from the cork, and trim the fabric leaving about 1/4 inch of extra fabric at the base of the crown. Stretch the brim over the crown and stick together with a little fabric glue. Trim any excess fabric.

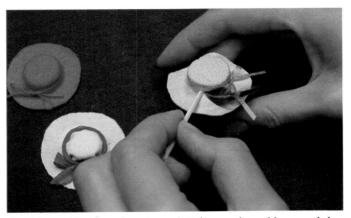

4 Brimmed hats can be trimmed with very thin ribbons and the tips of colored feathers, or they can be decorated with flowers. Bows can be made from ribbons and stuck onto the hats - when tying very small bows, it is easier to tie a normal-sized bow, and pull it through to make it smaller rather than trying to tie a tiny bow. Take the hat off the cork when you have decorated it.

Making a Hat Stand

1 Take a length of dowel 1/4 inch in diameter and, using a saw and miter box, cut one piece about 5 inches long, and three pieces 1/3 inch long (these will be the feet of the hat stand).

2 Mark the long piece of dowel with a pencil at 1 inch intervals from the top. Using the miter box and saw, score all around the pole on the pencil marks.

3 Sand the top of the pole so that it is rounded.

4 Using a bradawl, make three holes at an angle of 45 degrees to the pole on the top score mark. Make similar holes in the same positions on the third score mark, and in the middle, make holes in the opposite positions to those in the other two rows.

5 Take nine cocktail sticks, cut off the ends and cut them to just under 1 inch long. Sharpen one end with a craft knife.

6 Dab a little wood glue on the pointed ends, and stick the cocktail sticks into the holes on the pole.

7 Decide what shape you want to make the base of the stand and draw it onto balsawood ¼ inch thick. Score the shape with a craft knife, and cut it out. Cut the curves very slowly, paring a little away at a time, so that the wood doesn't split.

8 Sand down any rough edges of the base, and smooth the curves with sandpaper.

9 Make a hole in the bottom of the pole with a bradawl. Push a pin or a thin nail through the center of the base and into the hole in the pole. Dab a little wood glue on the base of the pole as well to reinforce it.

10 Stick the three feet onto the corners of the base with wood glue. Stick them right on the edges of the base so that part of the dowel sits outside the base.

11 Stain the hat stand with wood stainer or oil colors.

=========== **Assembling the Room** ===========

The hat shop wants to have plenty of accessories. Fill the shelves with rolls of fabric, ribbon and tulle - to make these, simply wind strips of fabric, tulle and ribbon around pieces of card. A feather jar is filled with the tips of colored feathers. The pin cushion is made by covering a ball of floral clay with fabric and sticking it to a washer. The pins in the pin cushion are very fine brass pins - cut them to about ¹/2 inch, and stick colored beads onto the ends with PVA adhesive. Dress the windows with hats and small stands. The small stands are made by sticking an upside-down golf tee into an acorn and painting it with oil paints. Trim the window ledge with sprigs of ivy (from doll house shops) which have been painted with gold varnish. The shelves are from doll house shops, but have been mahoganized and the glass-fronted cabinet is made from hardwood, which has also been mahoganized. The chaise longue has been reupholstered (see Yellow Drawing Room, page 35) with a subtle black-and-white striped fabric and a large gilt-framed mirror hangs on one wall.

FLOWER SHOP

One of the great things about doll houses is that if you get bored with the style of a room you can change or redecorate it very easily. The flower shop is being made in what was the Country Kitchen (see page 50). The rustic charm of the room is retained by keeping the beams in position, but otherwise it is completely transformed. A semi-circular shelved plant stand is covered with plants and flowers, and bunches of dried flowers hang on a rack and from the ceiling.

Walls and Ceiling

1 Pour some white distemper (if you haven't got distemper use matt white emulsion) onto a metal plate and tint it with Chinese orange, raw sienna and a tiny bit of burnt sienna to achieve a very pale pinky terracotta color.

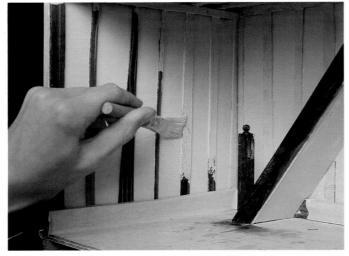

2 Apply the paint roughly to the walls and ceiling, including all the beams. Leave the stairs as they are. Paint it on roughly with a bristle brush so that the brush strokes show. Leave to dry. Apply a second coat if necessary, again quite roughly.

Making a Plant Stand

The plant stand, with four semicircular shelves fitted onto a freestanding triangular frame, is made from hardwood. The shelves can then be filled with pot plants.

1 Take a piece of hardwood $^1/_{16}$ inch and draw a semicircle with a diameter of $5^1/_4$ inches using a compass and pencil.

2 Again, using the compass and pencil, draw four concentric semicircles inside the first one. These semicircles are about $^5/_8$ inch wide, but the smaller semicircles should be narrower than the larger ones.

3 Cut out the semicircles with a very sharp craft knife. This is quite a tricky job and requires a lot of time and patience. Begin by scoring round the semicircles with the craft knife and then, very slowly and carefully, cut round them, a little bit at a time.

4 Smooth the circular edges with sandpaper.

5 Cut three strips of hardwood $^1/_{16}$ inch thick, each $4^1/_2$ inches long and $^1/_2$ inch wide for the 'legs' of the stand. Cut the bottom of each strip at an angle so they stand diagonally and join at the top to support each other.

6 Make three little nicks on the outside edges of all three strips, parallel to the base of the support, to support the shelves. Make sure that the nicks on the supports are at exactly the same height. The top shelf will be stuck on top of the supports; cut the top of each strip, parallel to the base, so that when the supports are stuck together, the top is horizontal.

7 Stick the supports together with wood glue. Stick the two back supports first, and then the perpendicular one.

8 Stick the shelves into the nicks on the supports with wood glue and stick the top shelf onto the top of the supports.

9 Stain the plant stand with a thin wash of green watercolor, so that the wood grain shows through.

Rack for Drying Flowers

1 Take a piece of hardwood ¹/₁₆ inch thick and draw out the shape of one side of the rack. I have drawn the side with one straight edge, and one curved double-bowed edge - you could simply draw a straight plank as the side of the rack.

2 Cut out the side of the rack using a very sharp craft knife. Place it on a piece of hardwood, draw round it and cut out the second side which will be exactly the same size and shape.

3 Make five holes in exactly the same positions on both sides of the rack with a bradawl.

4 Take five bamboo satay or kebab skewers and cut them to 4-inch lengths to make the poles across the rack. (The poles can be longer or shorter - it depends how wide you want the rack to be.) Sharpen the ends of each skewer with a pencil sharpener. Stick the skewers into the holes on one of the sides with wood glue. Then, stick the other ends of the skewers into the holes of the second side of the rack. Stain the rack with wood stainer.

Making Garden Statues

Statues can be made from plastic toy animals and people, wedding cake pillars and rectangular boxes. Simply stick the item onto a pillar or box, and paint the whole thing white.

Assembling the Room

The flower shop is filled with pot plants, dried flowers and statues. The potted geraniums on the plant stand are made from Fimo with florists-wire stalks. Hang the rack on the wall, hang baskets and trugs from the ceiling and put plenty of baskets and buckets of flowers on the floor. An oak table in the middle of the shop is loaded with more plants, a pair of miniature shears and any other suitable accessories.

5 Small dried flowers can now be tied onto the rack using very thin fuse wire. Flowers can be dried in any dry place such as a linen cupboard (you can also dry them in a microwave oven). Try to use a wide variety of dried flowers in different colors.

A THATCHED COUNTRY COTTAGE

It is remarkably easy to transform a fairly ordinary looking wooden doll house into a delightful flint cottage with a thatched roof. The materials are easily obtainable, and inexpensive - mop heads for the thatched roof, and gravel stones for the flint walls. You can also create a miniature fenced garden around the cottage.

Walls

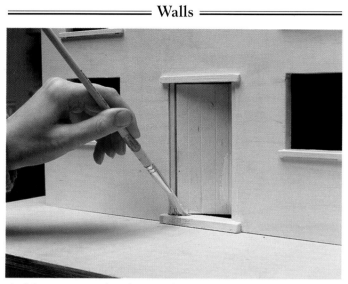

1 Mix a cream-colored primer by tinting white primer with a little raw umber gouache. Apply to the window sills, door, door frame and doorstep. Make sure that you paint the underside of the window sills. Leave to dry. Apply another coat if necessary.

2 Doll house and hobby shops sell sheets of bricks which can be cut out and stuck onto the outsides of houses. Cut out four strips of bricks, 2 bricks wide, to run up the corners of the cottage. Cut around the edges of the bricks to make them look realistic. Cut out strips of brick to go above each window and above the door. One edge will be straight, the other will be cut around the bricks - make these 1 brick high (i.e. every other brick will only be a half brick). Cut diagonal strips to go under the eaves of the house. These should be 1-1$\frac{1}{2}$ bricks wide and, again, one side will be straight. Finally, cut out bricks to cover the chimney stack, chimney pot and a little square with a hole in the middle to go on top of the chimney stack around the pot.

3 Mix some fine surface plaster filler with water, taking care to get rid of all the lumps. Filler tends to dry out after about 30 minutes, so only mix a quantity that you will use during that time. You can mix more later if you need it. Apply a layer of filler to the front of the house with a palette knife or a spatula. Apply it quite thickly, almost as though you were icing a cake, so that the stones can be pushed into it.

4 Stick the strips of brick onto the two front corners of the cottage and above the windows and door.

5 Starting at the bottom, stick the gravel stones into the filler. Use the flattest stones you can find. Gradually work your way up the front wall, until it is covered with stones. If the filler starts to dry out, add a little more to moisten the bottom layer.

6 When one wall is complete, repeat steps 3, 4 and 5 on the other three walls, one at a time. Don't forget to stick the bricks on the corners of each wall and under the eaves on the side walls. Leave overnight to dry and set.

7 Finally, stain the plaster with a dirty brown wash to give it an old and more weathered look. Add a little raw umber and black watercolor to a puddle of water on a tin plate, and mix it into a muddy brown glaze. Apply this glaze to each wall with a small, and preferably old, house paintbrush, making sure that you push the glaze into all the tiny gaps between the stones. Leave to dry.

Roof

The thatched roof is made from the strands of a mop head. You will need three or four mop heads. When you buy them you will see that there are different sorts - some have very thin strands, while others are really quite thick. Try to get ones with medium-sized strands.

1 Remove the metal clip from the mop head, and lay the strands out on the table.

2 Apply a generous coat of PVA glue to one side of the roof.

3 Starting at one end of the roof, lay the strands across the roof, pressing them into the glue. Make sure that you also stick some to the side edges of the roof. Separate the strands around the chimney and continue until this side is completely 'thatched'.

4 Fold the top of the strands back over upon themselves to create a fringe at the top of the roof. Secure any loose strands with more PVA.

5 Repeat steps 2, 3 and 4 on the other side of the roof.

6 Apply more PVA along the top of the roof where the two sets of thatch meet to reinforce them.

7 Trim the bottom of the thatch so that it hangs approximately $1/2$-$3/4$ inch below the bottom of the roof. You might have to trim it shorter around the upstairs windows.

8 Place a piece of paper under the top fringe. This fringe can be simply trimmed, or it can be a bit more interesting. I have made a zig-zag pattern, but you can do a wavy line or any other pattern. Repeat on the other side of the roof.

9 This is a pretty messy job, so before painting the thatch, it is a good idea to protect the cottage with sheets of newspaper. Mix some PVA with plenty of water in bowl. Add a squeeze of burnt umber watercolor, and a dash of black. Mix until you have a fairly dark, thatched-roof brown. Thin down with more water - the consistency should be very runny indeed. Using a small house paintbrush, and starting at the top of one side of the roof, apply the paint generously - it must soak right into the strands of the thatch - making sure that you don't leave any white patches. Repeat the process on the other side of the roof. Leave to dry.

Porch

The porch is made from a piece of lightweight cardboard with one straight edge, and one zig-zag edge, bent into a dome shape. Before marking out the card, it is best to experiment with paper to get the size of the zig-zags, and thus the size of the porch, right for your cottage. The zig-zags on the edges of the card need to be slightly wider than those in the center as they have to curve round further.

1 To make a porch, use a piece of medium-thick card - thick enough to be quite sturdy, but thin enough to bend easily. Mark out the zig-zag and cut it out using a craft knife and ruler.

2 Gently bend the cardboard into the domed porch shape. Staple the edges of the zig-zags together, starting at the bottom and working up to the top where all the tops of the zig-zags meet.

3 The porch is supported by two twigs which are about 1/2 inch wide. Cut them to the same height as the door.

4 Thatch the porch in the same way as the roof was thatched.

5 Stick the thatched dome onto the sticks with PVA adhesive. Finally, attach the whole porch to the cottage, and the bottom of the sticks to the ground with PVA adhesive.

The Garden

The garden path is made from sandpaper. Sandpaper comes in slightly different colors - try to get gravelly-colored sheets if possible.

1 Work out where the path is going to be - I have made it run down the sides and along the front of the cottage, with another path running from the front door to the gate. Cut out strips of sandpaper approximately 2-2½ inches wide to fit the paths.

2 Stick the sandpaper in position with rubber glue.

3 Cover any joins in the sandpaper by sticking little bits of lichen (from hobby shops) over the joins with rubber glue. It is also a good idea to stick lichen, as well as some miniature flowers, along the base of the cottage where the sandpaper doesn't quite fit under the stone walls. This also adds authenticity to the garden, since there are often weeds growing up through paths and around the edges of cottages.

The Lawn

1 To make the lawns in the front of the garden, you will need a bag of fine modeling turf (from hobby shops). The first step is to paint the area of lawn with green semigloss paint.

2 Sprinkle the 'grass' onto the paint, while it is still wet, so that it covers the paint in a thin, even layer and sticks to it. Leave to dry. Gently spray some hairspray or clear varnish onto the grass to stick it more firmly onto the paint base.

A Hanging Basket

To make a hanging basket to hang from the porch, you will need a piece of needlepoint canvas and a small bowl-shaped object such as a jewelry finding.

1 Wrap the needlepoint canvas around the jewelry finding and stick it down with PVA.

2 Stain the needlepoint canvas with burnt umber gouache.

3 Stick the ends of a length of thin cord or flower wire into the base of the basket with PVA.

4 Fill the basket with dried lichen and miniature flowers, and hang it from the porch.

The Fence

To make this you will need strips of hardwood ⅛ inch thick, some square dowel, and a bag of spills or tinder for lighting fires. The fence runs around the front and sides of the garden, with a gap in the middle where a gate will be placed.

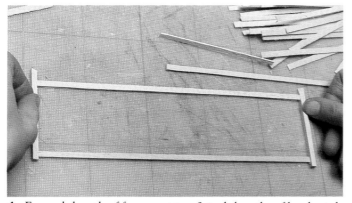

1 For each length of fence, cut two 3-inch lengths of hardwood for the vertical posts and two lengths of dowel for the horizontal supports. Stick the pieces of dowel between the posts to make the frame of the fence.

2 Cut the spills into lengths of approximately 3 inches - they need not be too exact. The tops of the spills should be broken at odd angles, so they look more realistic. Stick the spills onto the frame, approximately 1/3 inch apart with wood glue.

3 Apply a coat of white primer to the fence. Leave to dry.

The gate is made in the same way as the fence: make a frame from hardwood and dowel; stick the spills onto the frame, and finally stick one spill diagonally across the gate. Apply a coat of primer to the gate and leave to dry. Finally, stick the fence and gate to the base with PVA, and make a little rope loop to secure the gate to the fence.

The custom-made wooden doll house, before it was transformed.

Black Music Room

The style of this music room, which is adapted from Ravel's drawing room is early twentieth century. The effect of the black-and-white wall-to-wall carpet, daring for its time, is offset by the subtle elephant-gray striped wallpaper. It is a masculine room, with very little color. The furniture is Biedermeier style, with the chairs upholstered in rust silk which looks rich and old against the gray walls.

Walls and Ceiling

1 Apply a coat of white primer to the ceiling and to the walls, from the floor to the height at which a dado rail will be placed - about 2 inches above the floor. Leave to dry.

2 Apply a coat of white emulsion to the ceiling. Leave to dry.

3 Using a ruler, draw a pencil line across each wall 2 inches above the floor. This shows the position of the dado. Mix a dark gray paint, consisting of white semigloss tinted with burnt umber and black oil paints. Apply a coat of this paint to all the walls, from the floor to just above the pencil line. If any of the white undercoat shows through after the paint has dried, apply a second coat and leave that to dry.

The wallpaper for this room is a soft elephant-gray with black stripes. It is often quite difficult to find exactly the right wallpaper for a particular doll house room; sometimes full-size wallpaper can be used, but any pattern must be small enough to fit in with the scale of the room. Doll house shops sell special miniature wallpaper, but the range is not enormous. You might find wrapping paper with a suitable pattern, and be able to use that. If, however, you cannot find exactly what you want, it is quite easy to make your own wallpaper.

4 Mix some white poster paint with a little black, raw umber and burnt umber gouache to achieve a soft elephant-gray. Apply this to a sheet of construction paper, brushing it out in the direction that the black stripes will be drawn. Leave to dry.

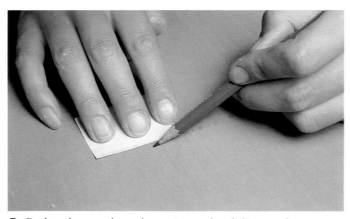

5 Rather than marking the position of each line on the gray paper, it is easier to mark them onto a piece of tracing paper or a Post-It note and use that as a template. You can then transfer the positions of a whole series of lines at once. A Post-It note is best because it sticks it to the paper, thus fixing its position. Either make up a pattern for the stripes or copy one out of a book and mark the positions of the lines on the Post-It note. Transfer them onto one end of the paper, and then move the Post-It note along to repeat the pattern right across the paper. Repeat the process at the other end of the paper so that the marks line up.

6 This stage needs to be done very carefully because if you make a mistake you will have to start again. Join up the marks using a metal ruler and a black felt-tip pen. It is important to draw the whole line at once, because putting the pen on and off the paper tends to leave a blob. Any blobs at the edges of the paper can easily be trimmed off.

7 Measure the height between the dado and the ceiling and mark the back of the wallpaper into a strip that will fit between them. Cut the paper with a scalpel or craft-knife, keeping the knife pressed right against the metal ruler.

8 Place the paper in the room and hold it against the wall. When it is in the right position, push it into the corners to make a fold in the paper and draw around the door and windows on the back of the paper. Cut around the door and windows with a pair of scissors or a scalpel and metal ruler. Rather than sticking the paper onto all three walls at once, it is easier to do two first and then the last one, so cut down one of the corner folds as well. (You may prefer to cut down both corner folds and stick each piece on separately.)

9 Stick 1/2-inch or 3/4-inch double-sided tape along each edge of the paper, around the edges of the door and windows, and on either side of the corner fold.

10 Take the piece of paper that will cover two walls, and starting on the side wall, stick it down, making sure that the paper goes right up to the ceiling. Work your way along this wall and onto the back wall, pushing the paper right into the corner at the back of the room. Stick up the second piece of paper on the other side wall in the same way. When all the paper is in position, trim any excess around the door and windows.

11 Cut lengths of cornice, baseboard and dado to fit the walls, and miter the ends. Spray a coat of gray primer to all these moldings and onto the door and door frame. Leave to dry, and then apply a coat of the gray paint used in step 3 below.

12 Stick the dado and cornice into the room. Do not stick the baseboard into the room until the carpet has been laid.

Floor

To make the black-and-white checked carpet you will need one piece of black cotton velvet, and one piece of cream-colored cotton velvet. If you cannot get cream velvet, buy white velvet, and dip it in cool weak tea to change the color to a creamy off-white.

1 Take a piece of thick construction paper. Put it onto the floor and mark out the exact dimensions of the room with a pencil.

2 Cut around the marks to create a template for the floor. If your room is square, draw in the two diagonals from the corners of the paper so that they cross in the middle of the template. If, however, your room is rectangular, mark off a square at one end of the rectangle, with one side of the square being equal to the shorter side of the rectangle. Draw in the diagonals.

3 Mark the backs of both pieces of velvet into square inches.

4 Cut the velvet first into strips and then into squares. Be very careful to cut along the weave of the fabric - this will ensure that the measurements are exact and that the squares are true and will join up properly; it will also stop the velvet fraying.

5 Using fabric glue stick the first velvet square onto the paper, with the corner of the square in the right angle formed by the two diagonals crossing. Then work your way out from the center, adding alternate-colored squares until the template is covered. The squares at the edges will hang over the sides of the paper - fold the extra fabric over and glue it onto the back of the paper.

6 Press the whole carpet with a cool iron; press it from the back to avoid crushing the pile of the velvet. Finally, stick the carpet onto the floor with PVA adhesive. Stick the baseboards onto the wall with wood glue.

Biedermeier Furniture

By repainting the woodwork, you can transform a very ordinary piece of furniture into one with the characteristic look of golden and black Biedermeier. If you are painting upholstered chairs, it may be easier to take off the arm rests and cushion so they don't get covered in paint.

1 Apply a coat of bamboo-colored semigloss paint to the furniture. Leave to dry overnight.

2 Pour a small puddle of semigloss varnish onto a metal plate. Place squeezes of raw sienna, lemon chrome and raw umber oil paints around the plate. Mix dabs of the colors into the varnish to achieve the dark honey color of Biedermeier (usually made from maple or satinwood). It is a good idea to have a picture of Biedermeier furniture as reference while you do this. You can check the color against the picture.

3 Apply a coat of the honey-colored varnish to all the furniture. Leave to dry overnight.

4 Finally, paint the black lines onto the furniture. Using a very thin 00 sable paintbrush and black semigloss paint, pick out any moldings on the furniture; if there are no moldings, pick out the edges of the pieces. When painting such fine lines paint with the side of the brush (i.e. run the brush along the shape of the wood) to get as straight a line as possible. Leave to dry.

Gilding a Picture Frame

Plastic picture or mirror frames can be bought from specialist doll house shops and then gilded with gold leaf.

1   Apply an even coat of one-hour gold size to the frame with a small sable brush. This is a very strong glue that needs to be left for an hour before sticking the gold leaf onto it. You can also buy three-hour gold size, which is left for three hours, or twelve-hour gold size, which is left for twelve hours. Make sure that you really cover the frame, getting it into all the moldings and returns.

2   After an hour the gold size should feel slightly sticky. Take a sheet of single fine gold transfer leaf, and cut it into strips that are slightly wider and longer than the sides of the picture frame. Books of gold transfer leaf can be bought in art shops - they come in different colored golds, but a good one to use is 'jaune'.

3   Press the gold leaf onto the frame and rub around all the moldings, and the edges of the frame. You might find it easier to use a cotton swab to get right round the moldings. When you have covered one side, lift the paper off - if there are any bits that have not been covered you can go over them again. Repeat this process on the other three sides of the frame.

4   Leave the frame for another hour so the size dries completely. Using a soft paintbrush, gently dust off any excess flakes of gold.

5   The gold frame will look very bright and shiny, so you need to distress it with a coat of dirty colored watercolor or gouache paint. Add burnt umber and black to water to get a good dirty brown, and add a tiny bit of dishwashing liquid to the paint - if you don't do this the paint will not stick to the gold frame. Paint it on with a small brush and leave to dry for half an hour.

If you don't want the frame to be gold all over, you could simply pick out the moldings in gold, or perhaps just have a gold line around the frame. Follow the same steps described above, but just apply the gold size to the areas that you want to be picked out.

Assembling the Room

Two simple corner bookcases (bought from doll house shops) fit into the back corners. Spray gray primer onto them, at the same time as priming the moldings (step 10 above), and paint them with the same gray paint as the moldings. Miniature porcelain and objets d'art are all available from doll house shops. However, you might like to try to make your own from Das or Marblex modeling clay. Similarly, it is more fun to make your own pictures, and gild your own picture frames. The musical instruments are from doll house shops.

NURSERY

The nursery is decorated in a traditional, almost Victorian manner. The colors are soft, muted pastels, the furniture is comfortable rather than fashionable and the room is littered with toys and games. It is Christmas, so there is a Christmas tree on the table, surrounded by presents, waiting to be opened, and cards, stuck onto ribbons, hang on the walls.

Walls and Ceiling

1   Apply white primer to the walls and ceiling and leave to dry.

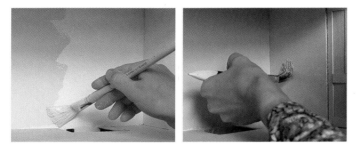

2   Mix a pale pink paint, consisting of white emulsion tinted with cadmium red, spectrum violet and raw sienna. Apply to one wall. Take a dry bristle brush with fairly stiff bristles and drag the brush through the paint in vertical strokes - this is known as dragging. Wipe the paint off the brush to keep it clean and dry. Repeat on the other walls, one at a time and leave to dry.

3   Cut lengths of cornice and baseboard to fit each wall of the room. Use a very simple cornice for the nursery. Miter the ends using a miniature miter box and saw (see page 11). Apply a coat of primer to these and to the door frame. Leave to dry.

4   Mix a little raw umber into some varnish, and apply a coat to the lengths of cornice, baseboard, and to the door frame - it will dry to give these an off-white, creamy tinge. Leave to dry.

5   Stick the cornice into the room with PVA or double-sided tape. Don't stick the baseboard in until the carpet has been laid.

6   Paint the fireplace black.

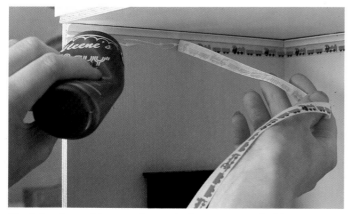

7   A border or frieze can be made from a piece of ribbon, or a strip of wrapping paper. If it is very white, stain it so that it is almost the color of the moldings - use tea to stain a fabric, or a coat of varnish tinted with raw umber to stain paper. Make sure that the pattern on the border fits the scale of the room - the border itself should be no deeper than 1 inch. Stick the border onto the walls, directly below the cornice, with all-purpose glue.

Making a Door

Although doll house shops sell doors, you may not always be able to find the right size, but it is not difficult to make your own.

1   Measure the size of the gap in the wall where the door will be placed - it is very important to do this accurately. Cut out a piece of hardwood $1/8$ inch thick to fit this hole exactly.

2   To create the panels of the door, you will need strips of hardwood $1/8$ inch thick and $1/2$ inch wide. Cut two lengths to fit the longest side of the door, using a miter box to get exact right angles. Sand down the ends so they are smooth. Stick them onto the door with wood glue.

3   Cut three lengths of hardwood to fit horizontally between the two verticals. Stick two at either end of the door, and the third about two-thirds of the way down the door.

4   Cut two more verticals to fit on either side of the middle horizontal. Stick them onto the door, so they run down the middle of the door, thus creating four panels.

5   Apply a coat of white primer to the door. Leave to dry.

6   Apply a coat of varnish tinted with raw umber (used in step 4 above) to the door to give it a creamy off-white color.

Floor

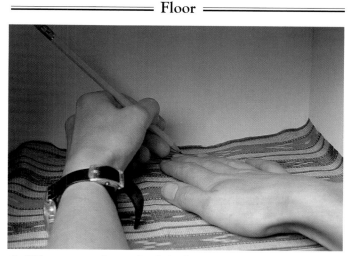

1 Take a piece of striped polished cotton, preferably with a slightly old and faded look. Place the fabric in the room and, with a pencil, mark the exact dimensions of the floor, together with the positions of the door, fireplace and stairs.

2 Cut out the fabric leaving an extra ¹/₄ inch all the way round to fold under - this will prevent any fraying. Fold over the ¹/₄-inch hem and stick it with double-sided tape. Stick the carpet into the nursery with double-sided tape.

3 Now you can stick the baseboard into the room with PVA or double-sided tape. Stick the door into the door frame, and stick the top of the banisters back into the room.

4 To make a throw rug to cover the carpet around the table, you will need a piece of heavy white or cream cotton. Cut it into a square or rectangle. Fold over a hem of approximately ¹/₄ inch, and stick it down with double-sided tape.

5 Attach the throw rug to the floor with small brass tacks. You might need to make small holes in the corners of the throw rug and in the floor so that the tacks can be pushed in more easily.

Christmas Cards

1 Cards can be made by cutting out pictures of Christmas cards from catalogues. Stick each one onto a piece of paper with paper glue. Cut and fold the paper so that it forms the back of the card. Vary the way the cards open - some sideways and some upwards.

2 Make a cord on which to hang the cards from a thin piece of colored ribbon. Tie a bow at the top and trim the loose end.

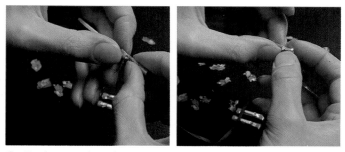

3 Stick the cards (use ones that open sideways) onto the ribbon with a tiny drop of glue on the inside of each card.

Party Snappers

1 Roll a piece of paper into a cylinder, and glue or sellotape it to keep it in this shape. Cut the cylinder into ³/₈ inch lengths.

2 For each snapper, cut a piece of silver or gold paper about 1 inch square. Roll it around the cylinder, keeping the cylinder in the middle, and secure it with a tiny blob of glue.

3 Stick a matchstick into one end, and pinch and twist the paper between the cylinder and the matchstick to make the end of the snapper - take care not to crush the paper. Repeat at the other end. Trim the ends of each snapper with red ribbon.

Christmas Tree

You can buy Christmas trees from doll house or model shops, or you can make them from real fir-tree sprigs - these will look more realistic.

1 Cut several sprigs from a fir tree with quite small needles. Bind them together with fuse wire or colorless nylon thread.

2 Tease and rearrange the sprigs into an even tree shape.

3 Put a blob of floral clay in a tub, and push the tree into it.

4 Paint the Christmas-tree tub with oil paints. Leave to dry and tie a ribbon into a bow around the tub.

5 Decorate the Christmas tree with tinsel - this is made by unraveling the strands of a steel wool pad and winding them loosely round the tree.

6 Candles are made by cutting little taper candles into $1/2$-inch lengths, and sticking them onto a sequin with PVA or Copydex. The sequin base can then be stuck to the tree with PVA.

7 Push small pins through tiny colored beads and stick them, and some small gold and silver stars, onto the tree with PVA.

Christmas Presents

1 Wrap little presents using the silver and gold paper from bars of chocolate or very small-scale patterned paper. Try to vary the shapes and sizes of the presents - you can use folded cardboard, scrunched-up bits of paper, and any small objects you can find.

2 Tie them up with very thin silk doll house ribbons.

Assembling the Room

Furnish the room with faded, comfortable-looking chairs. Cover the table with a Christmasy-looking cloth and put the table on the throw rug. The tree and presents can be placed on the table. Hang the Christmas cards on the walls, and also some nursery pictures. Scatter a few miniature toys, and perhaps a teddy bear in the room.

THE STUDIO AT CHARLESTON

Photographs in books and magazines are always a good source of ideas when you are decorating rooms in a doll house. It is also quite fun to find a photograph of a particularly unusual or spectacular room - a room in a stately home for example - and copy it as accurately as possible in your doll house. I have chosen Duncan Grant's studio at Charleston which is a very personal and eccentric room, and using a photograph as reference, I have reproduced it in miniature.

Walls and Ceiling

Before starting work on this room, stick masking tape all around the edges of the floor to keep it clean while the walls are being painted.

1 Apply white primer to the walls and ceiling. Leave to dry.

2 Cut out a simple shelf to fit around the chimney breast from hardwood 1/8 inch thick. The shelf should be about 1/2 inch wide. Sand down the corners so that they are rounded. Apply a coat of white primer to the shelf and, when it is dry, stick it around the chimney breast, about 5 inches from the floor.

The walls are painted with all sorts of dirty colors - the room is meant to look quite messy, so nothing needs to be very precise. Refer to your source picture constantly, and adapt the design if necessary to suit the shape of your doll house room.

3 Pour some white distemper onto a plate (if you don't have distemper use matt white emulsion). Tint the white paint with indigo, burnt umber and a little raw sienna gouache or water colors, and mix up the colors to achieve a dirty pale blue. Thin the paint down with water, until it is more of a wash. Using the photograph as a guide, apply the blue paint quite roughly to the appropriate parts of the walls - around the edges of each wall to create panels inside the blue paint. The brush marks should show, and the white undercoat should show through the wash.

4 Tint the blue paint with crimson and a touch of burnt sienna gouache or watercolor and add a little more white to achieve a pale pinky mauve color. Apply this roughly to the walls in the appropriate places - the panels on the side walls - again, allowing the brush marks to show. Keep the consistency of the paint very thin by adding more water if necessary.

5 Next, darken the paint with black to get a dark gray and paint this onto the panels on either side of the chimney breast.

6 Darken the paint further, watering it down if necessary, and paint the sides of the chimney breast. Also, paint the front of the chimney breast around the edges to frame a panel, which is square with a semicircle on top, above the fireplace.

7 Add more white distemper or emulsion to the paint, and more water if necessary, to achieve a pale gray. Apply this to the door, the inside of the fireplace and also to the arched part of the panel above the mantelpiece.

8 Add raw sienna and brilliant yellow to the paint to give a bright but dirty yellow, and apply to the chimney breast below the mantelpiece and to the two panels on either side of the pale gray arch above the mantelpiece. Lighten the yellow slightly and apply this paler paint to the top and bottom of each of the side panels above the mantelpiece, and also above the fireplace.

9 Finally, add more black and white to the yellow, to make a slightly yellowy gray. Paint a second arch above the mantelpiece, inside the pale gray one, leaving a pale gray border of about 1/2 inch. Also, apply this paint to the mantelpiece itself.

Floor

1 Remove the masking tape from the edges of the floor.

2 Mix 2-3 tablespoons of petroleum spirits with burnt umber oil paint in a paper cup. The mixture should be quite watery. This will be applied directly to the floor to stain the wood.

3 Test the color on a small part of the floor and adjust it if necessary - it should be a woody brown. When you are satisfied with the color apply the stain to the floor with a bristle brush, brushing it out in the same direction as the grain of the wood.

4 Leave it to dry for 30-40 minutes - the stain will soak right into the wood. Then, rub the surface with a cotton rag to remove any excess stain.

5 Thicken the petroleum spirits mixture by adding more burnt umber. Dip a bristle brush into the stain and, holding the brush over the floor in the hand you use for painting, gently draw your finger through the bristles of the brush to spatter the floor with tiny drops of this darker mixture. This will age the floor, and make it look dirtier and rougher.

6 When the floor has been well spattered, add black to the mixture to darken it further and repeat the process. Leave to dry.

Making Tables

It is important to get the right table for a particular room because tables are part of the character of that room - it is always worth consulting a few reference books to see what sort of tables suit the style of a room. They are relatively easy to make but quite expensive in shops. The painted tables for this room, which I have copied from the photograph of the room, are small, but the method for making them can be adapted to make any table - a large kitchen or hall table, or a console table, for example - simply by changing the size, height or shape of the table, and by using different thicknesses of wood and different-shaped legs.

1 First cut out the tops of the tables from hardwood 1/16 inch thick. I have cut out one top which is 1³/4 inches square, and one which is 1¹/2 x 2 inches.

2 Cut 1/8 inch dowel into 2¹/4-inch lengths for the legs.

3 Cut strips of hardwood 1/8 inch thick and 1/4 inch wide to make the horizontal supports underneath the table top. They should be slightly shorter than the sides of the table.

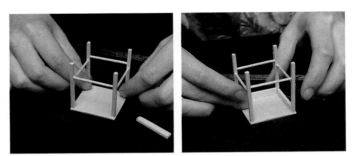

4 To make the lower supports between the legs, cut the pointed ends off cocktail sticks, and then cut them into lengths that are slightly longer than the top supports. Sharpen the ends of the cocktail sticks with a pencil sharpener or a craft knife.

7 Then, stick the tabletop onto the legs with wood glue. Finally, stick the top supports between the legs, directly beneath the tabletop, with a little wood glue.

If you are making a normal wooden table, you could simply stain it with wood stainer or petroleum spirits tinted with oil paints, but these tables are going to be painted to look like those in the photograph.

8 Apply a coat of white primer to the tables. Leave to dry.

5 Using a bradawl, make little holes in the legs about ¹/₂ inch up from the bottom to accommodate the horizontal supports. Each leg will have two holes on adjacent sides, although one will have to be slightly higher than the other.

9 Paint the tables, using those in the original picture as reference, with white distemper tinted with watercolors.

Fireplace and Chimney Breast

6 Next, stick the bottom supports into the holes in the legs with wood glue, so that the legs are all supported. The glue dries quite quickly so you will need to get all the parts in their correct positions within about 3-5 minutes.

1 Trace over the figures on the fireplace in the photograph of the real room. If they are not the right size, reduce or enlarge them on a photocopier. Transfer the tracings onto the fireplace.

2 Pour some white distemper or emulsion onto a plate and place squeezes of burnt sienna, black, raw sienna, ultramarine, and carthamus pink watercolors around the edge of the plate.

3 Add dabs of the watercolors to the white paint to achieve a flesh color, and paint in the bodies with this. Darken the flesh color slightly and paint in the shadows on the bodies. Keep adjusting the color slightly and build up the shadows of the bodies to make them look rounded. Outline the bodies in black.

4 Keep referring to the source picture, and paint in the rest of the decoration around the fireplace and above the mantelpiece, changing the color of the paint when necessary. You can either paint them on freehand if you feel confident and if they are quite easy, but if not, trace them first, reduce or enlarge the tracing on a photocopier and transfer them to the appropriate place.

Making Omega Pottery

1 Make miniature pots, vases and tiles from Fimo. Mold the Fimo into the appropriate shapes and bake them in a warm oven for 15-20 minutes.

2 Paint the pots and tiles with oil paints, using those in the photograph as reference.

Making a Screen

1 To make a screen with four panels you will need very thin hardwood 1/16 inch or thinner (use balsawood if you can't get hardwood thin enough) and a bag of twist ties for the hinges. Cut out eight pieces of hardwood, each 5 1/2 inches long and 1 3/4 inches wide. The screen is made by sticking these pieces of wood together with the food ties sandwiched between them.

2 Place the twist ties between the panels, about 1/2 inch from the top and bottom of each panel, and stick the panels together with wood glue (use PVA if the panels are balsawood). It is a good idea to place the whole screen under a weight or a heavy book for an hour or two so that it dries flat.

3 Apply white primer to the screen and leave it to dry. Paint the screen, using the screen in the photograph as reference, with white distemper or emulsion tinted with watercolors.

Assembling the Room

When you are furnishing the room, refer to the photograph for inspiration. The dirty wooden floor is partly covered by a large woven rug. Every possible surface in the room - tables, bookcases and even the mantelpiece - is crammed with plants, ceramics, books, lamps, and general clutter. The fabrics are faded chintzes, and the chairs are draped with pieces of brightly-colored cloth.

GROTTO

Inspired by photographs of a grotto in a German Baroque garden, the idea is to create a completely fantastical room. You can really let your imagination run riot here - nothing is too elaborate. It is a cavernous room, decorated almost entirely with shells. Before starting, you will need a large selection of small shells- these can either be collected from a beach, or bought from specialist shell shops. Try to get as many different-shaped shells as possible in strong contrasting colors such as red, white, black, brown and yellow to create a really strong and dramatic design.

Walls and Arch

The first stage in creating a grotto is to make the square room look cavernous - first by putting in a false arch at the front of the room, and then by making a curved back wall.

1 From three pieces of hardwood cut out a simple arch to fit the front of the room. Stick the three pieces of the arch together with wood glue. Sand down any rough edges.

2 Spray a layer of primer onto one side of the arch - make sure that you prime the rim of the arch as well. Leave to dry. Apply matt black paint to the front and rim of the arch.

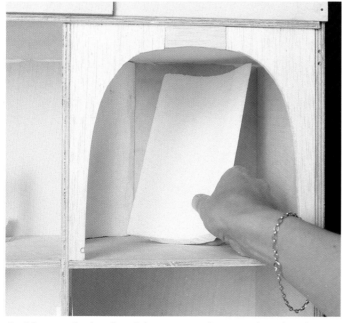

3 Measure the height of the room, and cut two lengths of polystyrene coving to fit from the floor to the ceiling. Using a very sharp scalpel, pare down both sides of the curves of the coving so that, when they are in position, they form a smooth curve with the back and side walls.

4 Take a large sheet of thin cardboard or thick construction paper, and cut one piece to fit the curved back wall, from the floor to the ceiling, and two pieces to fit the side walls. Don't forget to cut around any door or window frames.

5 Roughly apply a coat of buff-colored watercolor paint to the construction paper - don't worry if the brush marks show.

6 Darken your watercolor, and splash the darker paint onto the paper to give it a more textured look.

7 The next stage is to find designs that you can copy or adapt as a base pattern for each wall on which to arrange the shells. Books or magazines are a good source or you could, of course, design your own base patterns. Try to find patterns with curved lines that radiate out from a central point as this will help to emphasize the cavernous feel of the room.

8 If the designs are not the right size for your walls you can enlarge or reduce them on a photocopier. Trace the designs onto tracing paper. Hold the pieces of tracing paper in the room, to check that the designs suit the shape of the room. Once you are satisfied with them, transfer them to the buff-colored paper.

9 Before sticking any shells down, play around with the different shells on the pencilled patterns, until you have worked out a basic design. Try to contrast the colors and shapes of the shells as much as possible to achieve a very striking effect - if the colors of the shells are too similar, the pattern will not show up.

10 Once you have a sense of how the design will work, clear the shells off the paper, and spray the paper with a generous layer of Spray Mount. Now start sticking down the shells in place. Use tweezers to get the shells in the right position if necessary - fingers and thumbs might be a bit big and clumsy for this job.

11 Continue covering the designs with shells. If the Spray Mount dries and loses its stick, either spray on some more or reactivate it by warming the paper with a hairdryer - this will probably be necessary as shell-sticking is quite a time-consuming job.

12 When you have finished, sprinkle some sand and crushed shells over the paper to fill any gaps. Gently brush off any excess.

13 Finally, to fix the shells really securely to the paper, apply one or two coats of PVA adhesive mixed with water to each shell-covered piece of paper. PVA mixed with water also acts as a varnish so, when it dries, it will give the shells even more shine. Paint it on with a very soft nylon brush, and make sure that the PVA is pushed right around all the edges of the shells so that it seeps underneath them. Leave to dry.

Ceiling

1 Mix a dark midnight-blue paint, consisting of white emulsion tinted with indigo and burnt umber gouache. Thin the paint slightly by adding a little water.

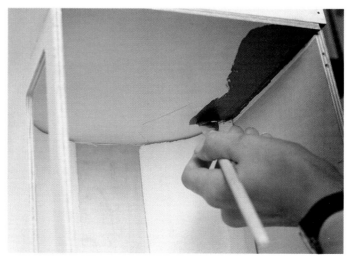

2 Test the color on the ceiling. It will look much darker when it is on the ceiling because it faces downwards and therefore there is no light on it. Apply an even coat to the ceiling.

Floor, Walls and Arch

1 Before sticking the shell-covered papers onto the walls, cut out a piece of lightweight cardboard or construction paper to fit the floor and stick it into the room with double-sided tape.

2 Apply an even coat of undiluted PVA adhesive to the walls and stick the paper onto the wall. Make sure that the paper on the back wall is properly centered, and push the paper right up to the ceiling and down to the floor. Leave to dry for two hours.

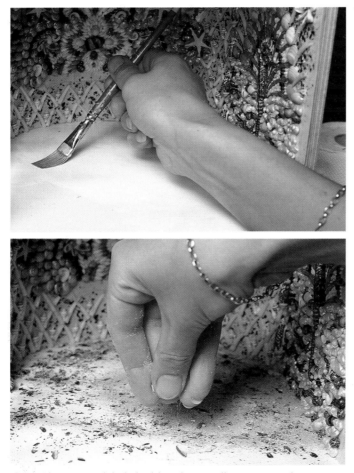

3 Paint a coat of slightly diluted PVA adhesive onto the paper on the floor. Sprinkle sand and crushed shells all over the paper - it is best to use strongly colored shells, black or red shells for instance, that will contrast well with the sand. Make sure that you sprinkle the sand right into the corners of the rooms, and that the whole floor is evenly covered. Leave to dry.

4 Brush off any loose sand or shells when the paper is dry.

5 Stick the arch into the front of the room with wood glue. Paint the rim of the arch with PVA and leave it for a few minutes - the adhesive becomes much stronger if left for a short while. Stick some tiny shells onto the rim, and hang some little tangled bunches of mussel shells from it.

Furniture

To make a chair you will need one complete flat shell such as a small scallop or small flat oyster and four long thin shells for the legs.

1 Separate the two halves of the flat shell, and glue the hinged edges together so they are at right angles to each other. Use a quick-setting epoxy resin glue. You will have to hold the shells in position until the glue has set - probably about five minutes.

2 Stick the four legs onto the base of the chair, again using rapid-setting epoxy resin glue.

3 A table is made in the same way as the chairs, using one flat shell for the tabletop and four thin shells for legs. Alternatively, you could make a table with a central pedestal, by sticking two or three stouter shells together, with a flat shell stuck on top.

The final step is to put all the furniture into the grotto, and add any finishing touches, such as a bottle of champagne in an ice bucket and glasses on the table.

DOLL HOUSE SUPPLIERS

With the increased popularity of making and decorating doll houses, there is now a huge number of specialist doll house shops and suppliers all over the country. Many of these are craftsmen specialising in just one tiny aspect of doll house decoration, while others are larger suppliers, selling a whole range of accessories. It would be impossible to list them all here but the most useful list of suppliers appears in an annual catalog produced by Kamblach Miniatures Inc, PO Box 1612, Waukesha, Wisconsin 53187 (tel: 414 769-8776). The National Association of Miniature Enthusiasts (NAME), PO Box 1178, Brea, CA 92622 publishes newsletters and organizes gatherings for doll house enthusiasts.

Photograph of Duncan Grant's studio at Charleston (page 64) by Howard Grey, from *Omega and After: Bloomsbury and the Decorative Arts* (Thames & Hudson).

Photograph of Schloss Regenau Coburg (page 118) reproduced by permission of the Royal Collection.

THE DECORATED DOLL HOUSE
Jessica Ridley

ERRATA, page 128:

The correct name and address of the company that produces an annual catalog is:

Kalmbach Miniatures, Inc.
PO Box 1612
Waukesha, Wisconsin 53187.

The correct telephone number for Kalmbach Miniatures is:

414-796-8776.

The publisher regrets any inconvenience these errors may cause.